I0761323

**Radio's Revolution**

# Radio's Revolution

## Don Hollenbeck's *CBS Views the Press*

Edited and with an introduction by Loren Ghiglione

UNIVERSITY OF NEBRASKA PRESS | LINCOLN AND LONDON

*Library of Congress Cataloging-in-Publication Data*
Radio's revolution: Don Hollenbeck's CBS views
the press / edited and with an introduction by
Loren Ghiglione.
p. cm.
Includes bibliographical references and index.
ISBN 978-0-8032-6758-9 (cloth: alk. paper)
1. CBS views the press. 2. Hollenbeck, Don.
3. United States—Politics and government—
1945–1989.
I. Ghiglione, Loren.
PN1991.77.C44R33 2008
791.44'72—dc22 2008024045

Set in New Baskerville.
Designed by Ashley Muehlbauer.

*To Rae Whitney Ghiglione*

# Introduction

*CBS VIEWS THE PRESS* ranks as one of the most important radio programs in U.S. journalism history.[1] The pet project of Edward R. Murrow, vice president in charge of news and public affairs at the Columbia Broadcasting System, the fifteen-minute program aired over WCBS in New York City on Saturdays at 6:15 p.m. from 1947 to 1951.[2] The program dared to declare radio's independence from newspaper, the dominant news medium in America for more than 250 years.

In 1947 a network decided for the first time it wasn't only going to be a target of newspapers' critics. Instead, CBS chose to use its team of correspondents to evaluate and criticize the reporting by New York's major metropolitan newspapers. *CBS Views the Press* gave radio journalists a voice they had not used before to critique a news medium not known for self-doubt or self-criticism.

The newspapers examined each week by *CBS Views the Press* represented the full range of financial health, history, and political ideology. New York City newspapers on the left included the *Daily Worker*, the propaganda sheet of the Communist Party; Dorothy Schiff's ancient afternoon *Post* (founded by Alexander Hamilton in 1801); and the ad-free, photo-rich *PM*, an experimental tabloid (1940–48) that would be reborn under new ownership as the *Star* (1948–49) and then the *Compass* (1949–52). More to the right were two afternoon newspapers: Scripps Howard's *World-Telegram* and the *Sun*, with its "better-able-to-buy" subscribers.[3] Scripps Howard purchased the corpse of the *Sun* in 1950 to form the *World-Telegram and Sun*.

Other New York City newspapers were powerhouses of the U.S. press. The *New York Times* ranked among the world's most prestigious newspapers. The *Herald Tribune*, which claimed Horace Greeley as its founder, competed with the *Times*, but the death of editor/owner Ogden Reid and the appointment as editor of his son, thirty-three-year-old Whitelaw Reid, in January 1947 perhaps marked the beginning of the *Tribune*'s two-decade-long demise. The tabloid *Daily News*, a picture paper filled with comic strips, sensationalism, and sex, had the largest circulation of any U.S. paper, over two million. William Randolph Hearst's tabloid *Mirror*, with the nation's second-largest circulation, and his flagship *Journal-American*, the city's largest-circulation afternoon paper, served as the conservative mouthpieces of America's mightiest media baron.

Murrow chose Don Hollenbeck, a forty-two-year-old CBS correspondent, to write and narrate *CBS Views the Press* and to coordinate the network's correspondents from around the globe who contributed to the program. Hollenbeck, in turn, helped select two seasoned journalists with newspaper experience, Joseph Wershba and Edmund Scott, to work with him.

Hollenbeck had the appearance of a young Abe Lincoln before the future president grew a beard—dark-haired, heavy browed, thin (only 150 pounds on a nearly six-foot frame), almost frail.[4] But Murrow knew Hollenbeck had a spine of steel. He was willing to report on McCarthyism years prior to the word's invention. He was also willing to be honest in his criticism, whatever the retaliatory name-calling—and pressure on CBS as well as on him—by publishers and editors.

Hollenbeck sounded like the *New York Times*. He always seemed under control, however disturbing the topic, and oozed authoritativeness. And he could write clear, concise essays that were memorably eloquent. Fred Friendly, president of CBS News from 1964 to 1966, described Hollenbeck as "one of the few great writers that broadcasting has produced."[5]

Hollenbeck also knew the press, both print and broadcast, from the inside. After attending the University of Nebraska, he began reporting in 1926 for the major daily newspaper in his hometown, the *Journal* of Lincoln, Nebraska, and married the majority owner's daughter, Jessie Seacrest. In 1929, after a divorce from Seacrest, he moved to Omaha to work as a reporter, then an "ace feature writer," and finally book editor/night editor for Hearst's *Bee-News*.[6] When the *Bee-News* was sold to the *Omaha World-Herald* in 1937, Hollenbeck moved to his long-time Omaha rival. But within weeks, at a time when photojournalism was transforming newspapers and magazines, he landed a photo-desk position at the Associated Press in New York.

Victor Haas, a *Bee-News* reporter, said Hollenbeck "belonged to New York City. All of Nebraska was just a stopping-off place for Don. He was always reading books that most of the journalists couldn't understand anyway."[7] Hollenbeck and his second wife, Mildred Raleigh, whom he would divorce in three and a half years, moved to Manhattan.

In 1940 he was one of approximately two hundred journalists selected from eleven thousand applicants to launch *PM*, an innovative, photo-laden tabloid staffed by Margaret Bourke-White and other world-class photographers and called "the first new idea in American newspapering since the penny press."[8] Drawing on his experience at the AP, he joined the paper as an assistant photo editor. After a brief stint at NBC as a radio news writer, he returned to *PM* in the summer of 1941 as a national-affairs editor.

He reported on politics and wrote pithy editorials. While left of center, *PM* early championed U.S. entry into World War II and aggressively supported the Allied cause. When the federal government announced regulations requiring that more biscuits, pemmican, and other emergency rations be carried in lifeboats aboard U.S. ships, Hollenbeck's brief editorial commended the requirements but ended tartly, "You can't sink a Nazi submarine with an Army biscuit or Navy pemmican, no matter how solid they are. Where in the hell are the guns that the Navy was ordered to put aboard those ships?"[9]

With the entry of the United States into World War II, many talented *PM* journalists enlisted in the army or joined the Office of War Information. Hollenbeck took an editing position with the OWI in London. But radio news attracted him. The public put more faith in radio reporting than in newspaper coverage of World War II by better than two and a half to one.[10] Stanley Richardson, head of the NBC bureau in London, hired Hollenbeck as a 125-dollar-a-week war correspondent in February 1943. *Stars and Stripes* described Hollenbeck's coverage of the Allied landing at Salerno, Italy, later that year as "one of the most dramatic recordings we've ever heard. Against a backdrop of gunfire Don gave a vivid description of the bitter battle raging about him."[11]

Despite his talent, Hollenbeck was a reluctant witness to war. Recovering from malaria and jaundice, Hollenbeck persuaded NBC to return him to New York in January 1944. When NBC transferred Hollenbeck back to Europe in August 1945 to cover the Nuremberg war-crimes trials and other postwar news, the depressed correspondent wrote to his third wife, Anne, about wanting to quit NBC and return to New York to be a newscaster, newspaper editor, or bookstore owner. Anne, as well as Hollenbeck's agents, Tom Stix and John Gude, advised against such a rash course. But a bored, lonely Hollenbeck, "fed up with death and destruction," gave away his correspondent's uniform and flew home.[12] NBC fired him.

ABC soon hired Hollenbeck to broadcast the news over WJZ, its New York City station. Hollenbeck earned the applause of ABC executives—and the honor of substituting for vacationing Raymond Gram Swing, an evening coast-to-coast commentator—until he responded on air to a singing commercial that preceded one of his 7:00 a.m. WJZ broadcasts.

On August 14, 1946, after looking at his script about rioting in Haifa, a UN dispute, and other life-and-death topics, then listening to the commercial about the man with the Marlin Blades shave ("He makes all the ladies rave woo-woo!"), Hollenbeck growled into the microphone, "The atrocity you have just heard is no part of this show."[13] ABC fired him three hours later.

So when Murrow hired Hollenbeck in 1946 and soon chose him to broadcast *CBS Views the Press,* he knew he was hiring a principled, if impulsive, two-decade veteran of the news media.

*CBS Views the Press* was Murrow's favorite child—the radio program in which he "took the sharpest interest and for which he had felt the greatest need," recalled CBS broadcaster Alexander Kendrick.[14] Hollenbeck knew that. As is evident in the twenty broadcast transcripts in this book, Hollenbeck made sure that *CBS Views the Press* tackled the toughest, most controversial postwar subjects, from racism to McCarthyism, and that it ranked with the best radio programs being aired. *CBS Views the Press* won George Peabody, George Polk, and many other major journalism awards.

Less than four months after Hollenbeck began his *CBS Views the Press* program, Murrow resigned as the network's vice president in charge of news and public affairs to return to broadcasting. Murrow lobbied CBS president Frank Stanton to continue to protect Hollenbeck's *CBS Views the Press.* But in early 1950, the network's management replaced Hollenbeck, a brave iconoclast, with Douglas Edwards, a corporate conformist.

Of his departure, Hollenbeck publicly said, "An increase of work makes it impossible to do full justice to a program which requires as much concentrated effort as this one does."[15] He began emceeing *We Take Your Word,* a radio panel show about the meaning of words. He continued to play at-the-scene reporter for radio re-creations of historical events on *You Are There.* Later, he started participating in the *Hear It Now* news program of Murrow and Fred Friendly that would eventually evolve into *See It Now* on television.

Despite Hollenbeck's public statement, CBS veterans were convinced that Hearst and other powerful media bosses whose newspapers were the targets of Hollenbeck's criticism pressured CBS to remove Hollenbeck and gut the program. Edwards was to "'featurize' rather than criticize," recalled CBS News writer Jack

Walters.[16] Within a year, Edwards's timid version of *CBS Views the Press* died quietly.

Still, the memory of Hollenbeck's broadcasts kept alive the idea of someday reviving his kind of principled *CBS Views the Press.* CBS chairman William S. Paley said that he personally persuaded correspondent Charles Collingwood, reluctant to move from the network to a local station, to undertake a televised fifteen-minute version of *CBS Views the Press* for New York's WCBS in 1961.[17] The message was, Collingwood recalled: "What we want to do is encourage the five CBS-owned-and-operated stations to look at the press in their own areas, and then possibly we'll go to the network with the pattern of Hollenbeck's program."[18] *WCBS-TV Views the Press* had a short, unhappy life.

Later, CBS broadcast a snippet of media criticism nationally during *CBS Morning News.* And CBS correspondent Mike Wallace, who saw Hollenbeck as a hero, tried unsuccessfully to sell Don Hewitt, producer of *60 Minutes,* on occasionally running a Hollenbeck-style segment of press commentary on that program.[19]

None of the efforts measured up to Hollenbeck's *CBS Views the Press.* To Paley, Hollenbeck's *CBS Views the Press* represented a golden moment in the network's history. "He set a very high standard," Paley said. "We never could find anybody after that we thought could do such a good job." Paley, however, failed to understand the reasons for Hollenbeck's success, repeatedly mentioning only the broadcaster's neutrality. "He was an honest man who tried to look at things objectively," Paley said. "He wasn't out to get anybody, he was out to do an objective job in reviewing what the press was doing."[20]

But some of what Hollenbeck achieved was what Paley and other network bosses opposed. They worried not only about rancorous, ruthless partisanship but also about any analysis by newscasters. Less than a month before Hollenbeck's death, Paley spoke to the National Association of Radio and Television Broadcasters about "the road to responsibility." He insisted that broadcasters had the same right as print journalists to independent expression.

In the next breath, however, he said, "I am not urging anyone to exercise this right."[21]

Others understood that an unexercised right inevitably turns into a nonexistent right. John Crosby, a noted radio and television critic, decried the absence of independent expression in television news and hoped optimistically that *CBS Views the Press* would be "the forerunner of other programs of the same style and with as much integrity."[22]

CBS radio veteran Robert Lewis Shayon, who became a *Saturday Review of Literature* radio and television critic, also called on news producers to allow a point of view in broadcasts—"any point of view so long as it is honest, creative, responsible, and courageous. I have in mind . . . the kind of job Don Hollenbeck used to do on *CBS Views the Press.* But that kind of job takes not only money and time—it takes thought; and that's a dimension that's sort of scarce around the networks these days."[23]

Fueled by a hair-trigger impetuousness as well as a willingness to be different, Hollenbeck stretched to its outermost limit the second-class First Amendment permitted by the networks, which were afraid to allow analysis and opinion that might anger the public and threaten stations' highly profitable licenses to broadcast. While never blatantly abusing the networks' rules against the broadcasting of opinion, Hollenbeck "said what he wanted to say," CBS newscaster Alan Jackson recalled. Jackson described Hollenbeck as "always outspoken" during a time when outspokenness was not a quality embraced by CBS's bosses.[24]

On March 9, 1954, Murrow used his half-hour *See It Now* broadcast to examine the record of Senator Joseph McCarthy, a demagogic anti-Communist crusader. Film showed McCarthy belittling President Eisenhower; attacking "Alger, I mean Adlai" Stevenson, former Illinois governor and unsuccessful Democratic Party presidential candidate; and labeling General Ralph Zwicker, who was a hero of Normandy and the Bulge in World War II, "a disgrace to the army." Murrow ended the program with an eloquent call for action: "This is no time for men who oppose Senator McCarthy's methods to keep silent or for those who approve. . . . We proclaim ourselves, as indeed we are, the defenders of freedom—what's left of it—but we cannot defend freedom abroad by deserting it at home."[25]

At 11:00 p.m., a few seconds after Murrow finished, a delighted Hollenbeck came on the air in New York for his WCBS newscast. Hollenbeck did not "keep silent." He told his WCBS audience, "I don't know whether all of you have seen what I just saw, but I want to associate myself and this program with what Ed Murrow has just said, and I have never been prouder of CBS."[26]

With that one sentence, Hollenbeck put his career—and, it turned out, his life—at risk. CBS's Collingwood recalled the network's reaction to Hollenbeck's extemporaneous remark: "This was taken as a sign of almost unprofessionalism. There was a kind of growing tension between Hollenbeck and management: his own personality—not letting anyone kick you around—plus his taking . . . chances."[27] CBS's Friendly said, "CBS was not as courageous as it could have been. Someone made the decision that Don was expendable."[28]

McCarthy's defenders attacked Hollenbeck. Jack O'Brian, a bullying radio and television critic of Hearst's *Journal-American*, had never forgiven Hollenbeck for his *CBS Views the Press.* O'Brian labeled it a "program of criticism of conservative newspapers"[29] and used his *Journal-American* column to bludgeon Hollenbeck repeatedly. O'Brian cast Hollenbeck as the "stern, intense type, [having] a messianic mien and a habit of baiting Dixiecrats and conservatives with blandly phrased 'loaded' questions."[30]

Murrow told Hollenbeck not to worry about O'Brian's attacks. Hollenbeck should try to ride out the storm, Murrow said. But a depressed Hollenbeck despaired. Separated from his third wife, Anne, he drank too much, fretted about their adopted daughter, Zoë, feared CBS would fire him, and recalled how his mother had died—by slitting her jugular with her husband's razor. In the early morning of June 22, 1954, Hollenbeck, wearing shorts and a bathrobe, turned on the four burners and oven jet of his apartment stove, sat on a hassock in his kitchenette, and leaned back against the wall. He waited for the closed kitchenette to fill with gas and kill him.

Death by suicide is invariably caused by many factors, including depression. But Hollenbeck's colleagues at CBS blamed O'Brian. CBS News anchor Walter Cronkite described O'Brian as "a McCarthyite Red-baiter who had the distinction, as far as we at CBS News were concerned, of having hounded to a suicide's grave one of our most distinguished reporters." O'Brian "was really a very bad man," Cronkite said.[31]

The *New York Post*'s Jay Nelson Tuck, recalling that *CBS Views the Press* had "found the weak points of the Hearst papers," suggested O'Brian and other Hearst writers had never forgotten. In his *Post* column, Tuck said he had twice almost told the story of O'Brian's "persistent campaign" to drive Hollenbeck off the air. But Hollenbeck had requested his friend withhold the story. Hollenbeck felt it better, Tuck said, "not to be enticed into a gutter fight."[32] Hollenbeck said he would attempt to ride out O'Brian's smear campaign, including O'Brian's request for letter writers to Red-bait Hollenbeck. Even after Hollenbeck's death, O'Brian published a column that smeared him as "one of the most prominent members of the CBS lefties, and he hewed to its incipient pink line without deviation."[33]

The night after Hollenbeck's death, Murrow ended his *See It Now* telecast with a tribute to his friend: "One of the best programs I ever heard was called *CBS Views the Press.* A great many people liked it; some didn't. No one ever said it was anything but honest. It was the work of an honest reporter, Don Hollenbeck. . . . He had been sick lately, and he died this morning. The police said it was suicide—gas."

When Murrow got to the word "gas," his stern, stoic face momentarily lit with emotion. His lower lip appeared to disappear under his upper lip. Then, as if talking to O'Brian, Murrow looked straight in the camera and said, "Not much of an obit." He finished speaking without looking again at his script, "But at least we had our facts straight, and it was brief, and that's all Don Hollenbeck would have asked."[34]

## Notes

1. The *CBS Views the Press* transcripts are available in the University of Nebraska–Lincoln Libraries, Archives and Special Collections, Don Hollenbeck, Broadcast Papers (MS 319); and Columbia University, Butler Library.
2. Bob Edwards used the term "pet project" in *Edward R. Murrow and the Birth of Broadcast Journalism* (Hoboken NJ: John Wiley and Sons, 2004), 94.
3. Advertisement for the *New York Sun*, *Editor & Publisher*, January 19, 1947, 17.
4. The comparison to a young Abe Lincoln is made by Joseph Wershba in his recollection of a conversation with Lincoln historian and poet Carl Sandburg, as recorded on "A Tribute to Zoë," a 1950 "collection of sounds" made by Don Hollenbeck about his career for his six-year-old daughter, Zoë. The "Tribute to Zoë" records are in the University of Nebraska–Lincoln Libraries, Archives and Special Collections, Don Hollenbeck, Broadcast Papers (MS 319).
5. Fred Friendly, interview with editor, July 8, 1975, New York.
6. The *Omaha Bee-News* billed Hollenbeck as its "ace feature writer" in promoting a 1937 series he wrote that was reprinted and distributed as "What Parents Should Know About Our Schools." A box of twenty clippings from the series, published between January 29 and February 19, 1937, are in the University of Nebraska–Lincoln Libraries, Archives and Special Collections, Don Hollenbeck, Broadcast Papers (MS 319).
7. Victor Haas, interview with editor, April 24, 1975, Omaha NE.
8. J. Anthony Lukas, "Where Are You Now, PM Spinney?" *New Republic*, September 9, 1972, 27.
9. Don Hollenbeck, "They Ask For Guns, They Get Pemmican," *PM*, January 23, 1942, 3.

10. This 1942 government-sponsored poll is cited in Mark Bernstein and Alex Lubertozzi, *World War II on the Air: Edward R. Murrow and the Broadcasts That Riveted a Nation* (Naperville IL: Sourcebooks, 2003), 219.
11. *Stars and Stripes*, September 20, 1943, as quoted in "War Correspondents in Person" in Hollenbeck scrapbook, 68, Don Hollenbeck, Broadcast Papers (MS 319), Archives and Special Collections, University of Nebraska–Lincoln Libraries (hereafter cited as Hollenbeck scrapbook).
12. Don Hollenbeck to Anne Hollenbeck, August 26, 1945, Don Hollenbeck, Broadcast Papers (MS 319), Archives and Special Collections, University of Nebraska–Lincoln Libraries.
13. As quoted in "Off Pitch," *Time*, August 26, 1946, 56.
14. Alexander Kendrick, *Prime Time: The Life of Edward R. Murrow* (Boston: Little, Brown and Company, 1969), 299.
15. As quoted in Ralph Leviton, "Myopia at CBS," *News Workshop*, undated clipping in Hollenbeck scrapbook, 137.
16. Jack Walters, interview with editor, August 5, 1975, New York.
17. William S. Paley, interview with editor, February 16, 1977, New York.
18. Charles Collingwood, interview with editor, August 5, 1975, New York.
19. Mike Wallace, interview with editor, August 15, 2005, Vineyard Haven MA.
20. William S. Paley, interview with editor, February 16, 1977, New York.
21. William S. Paley, *1974/1954: Free Broadcast Journalism* (N.p.: CBS, 1974), 26. See also Sally Bedell Smith, *In All His Glory: The Life of William S. Paley, the Legendary Tycoon and His Brilliant Circle* (New York: Simon and Schuster, 1990), 364–65.
22. John Crosby, "A British Opinion of Us," *New York Herald Tribune*, 1947 clipping in Hollenbeck scrapbook, 57.
23. Robert Lewis Shayon, "Scraps of Sound and History," *Saturday Review of Literature*, February 10, 1951, 30.
24. Alan Jackson, interview with editor, January 25, 1975, New York.
25. *See It Now*, March 9, 1954. A broadcast tape is available in the CBS News Archives, New York.

26. As quoted in Fred Friendly, *Due to Circumstances Beyond Our Control* . . . (New York: Vintage Books, 1967), 41.
27. Charles Collingwood, interview with editor, August 5, 1975, New York.
28. Fred Friendly, interview with editor, July 8, 1975, New York.
29. Jack O'Brian, "Rep. Hill Labels CBS a Supporter of Leftist Trends," *New York Journal-American*, July 26, 1951, 26.
30. Jack O'Brian, "O'Brian Holds Caucus on TV Commentators," *New York Journal-American*, July 28, 1952, 23.
31. Walter Cronkite, interview with editor, October 11, 2005, New York.
32. Jay Nelson Tuck, "Don Hollenbeck," *New York Post*, June 23, 1954, 4, 72.
33. Jack O'Brian, "Continuing Study of the Continuing CBS News 'Slant,'" *New York Journal-American*, June 23, 1954, 37.
34. *See It Now*, June 22, 1954. A broadcast tape is available in the CBS News Archives, New York. Murrow's tribute to Hollenbeck from that broadcast is also quoted in Friendly, *Due to Circumstances Beyond Our Control* . . . , 64.

## Editor's Note

Hollenbeck's writing for radio relied on numerous dashes to mark his on-air pauses. While those dashes normally might be converted into semicolons in published transcripts, I have kept some of the dashes and replaced others with periods and colons, as well as semicolons, to avoid a sea of semicolons. Semicolons are "transvestite hermaphrodites representing absolutely nothing," Kurt Vonnegut wrote. "All they do is show you've been to college."

Radio's Revolution

# May 31, 1947

Don Hollenbeck's first broadcast established the format, focus, and voice of *CBS Views the Press.* The program's voice was that of an authoritative, fair, no-nonsense skeptic. The voice's toughness may have owed a debt to a suggestion by Hollenbeck's boss, Edward R. Murrow, to send a first draft of the broadcast's script to *Herald Tribune* columnist John Crosby for his comment. Crosby, a friend to both Hollenbeck and Murrow, recommended Hollenbeck give the broadcast a harder edge. Hollenbeck did so, describing the critical coverage by New York papers of welfare families' temporary residence in hotels as a "newspaper lynching party." Hollenbeck's focus over the two and a half years of his *CBS Views the Press* was on media abuse of the vulnerable and defenseless. He returned to the hotel relief story a dozen times. The first broadcast also established the program's usual format: a main story followed by several brief laurels and darts. Reaction to Hollenbeck's program ranged from rave reviews to a Red-baiting rebuke. Writers for *PM,* the *Herald Tribune,* and other newspapers praised the program's courage and discretion. A trade magazine quoted Keats Speed, executive editor of the *Sun,* as saying, "Several newspapers follow the Communist line, so why shouldn't a radio station?"[1]

THE GREAT INK-LETTING which resulted from the disclosure that a number of New York City families on relief had been housed in hotels has abated some, after having for about a week resembled a kind of newspaper lynching party. The immediate victims were 37 families, representing about 120 persons, who had been housed in hotel rooms by the city's Department of Welfare on the ground that it had been unable to provide adequate shelter for them elsewhere.

1. "CBS Station in New York Starts Criticism of Press," *Editor & Publisher,* June 7, 1947, 11.

May 31, 1947

The lynching was a success—if you can call a lynching a success. The families have been hustled from their hotel rooms; at first they were put into condemned tenements and the city lodging houses, of which more later. All in all, it was about as sorry an exhibition as the press—or a section of it—is capable of putting on. It began in the *World-Telegram*, under circumstances in themselves extremely interesting and which will be discussed later. The stories told how some relief families were being supported in what was made to sound like the lap of luxury, living in what were described as midtown, Herald Square, and Murray Hill hotels and apparently drawing checks of fantastic proportions every month. The story was quickly taken up by every newspaper in town, from one point of view or another. It was one of those things which couldn't be ignored. It even got into vaudeville: Jack Benny opened his stage show at the Roxy, and one of his jokes was that he was being treated so handsomely at the Sherry-Netherland Hotel that people thought he was on relief.

In the *News*, Danton Walker wrote, and I quote, "New York's current charity scandal at least helps explain the shortage of hotel rooms, according to the Broadway wags." Those Broadway wags are never at a loss for a wisecrack. All is grist for their mills—even misery. And the impression of some extremely fancy living by the relief clients was what you might have gained by reading the accounts in just one section of the press. The *Sun*, for instance, took the story to its heart after the *World-Telegram*'s disclosure and really went to town, closely followed by the *Journal-American*. The *Sun* did several stories on the situation. One of them, written by Charles Wyer, quoted several unidentified persons—unidentified because Mr. Wyer wrote that they were so close to the city's relief picture that their names could not be used for obvious reasons. But Mr. Wyer went on to quote his anonymous informants as saying, among other things, that the Welfare Department has made public assistance far more attractive to thousands of persons than jobs. Also—and this is a grave accusation—that it is almost a general rule, according to anonymous information obtained by the *Sun*, to give out money to those who ask for it, sometimes two hundred dollars at a clip, and ask questions afterward. Another story in the *Sun*, this time by Phelps Adams of the newspaper's Washington bureau, referred to "scores" of families being lodged in midtown hotels, complete with maid service. This maid service touch, by the way, appeared to fascinate the *Sun* staff.

In three stories within two days, it was carefully pointed out that the relief clients were getting maid service; the impression was that most hotels don't supply it to their guests. Other writers of these relief stories seemed impressed by the fact that the relief guests had radios in their rooms. The unuttered question was, what are THESE kinds of people doing with maid service and radios? The *Journal-American* was a little slower getting started than the *Sun* was, but when it did, it also referred to the Welfare Department's policy of handing out large sums of money first and asking questions afterward. Not even anonymous authorities were called in to back up the *Journal-American*'s statement, but the wording of its story was strikingly similar to that of the *Sun*'s account the evening before.

Both the *Sun* and the *Journal* hinted at Communist conniving in the affair, and both papers referred to Communists occupying key positions in the Welfare Department. This phase the *Journal* hit hard and in red ink. Another paragraph in a *Sun* story said, to quote part of it, "Relief is doled out to refugees landing here from day to day from foreign ports and to Puerto Ricans who flock to New York in large numbers, armed with the knowledge that the city of New York is generous to a fault, perhaps, to those in need." Mr. [Edward E.] Rhatigan, the commissioner of welfare, had to straighten the *Sun* out on that one. He explained that in the past three years, 2,005 repatriated Americans had been cared for by the Welfare Department and that the city had been reimbursed for its expense by the federal government.

Almost lost sight of in the storm and strife over the story was the fact that the great majority of the 233,000 persons on New York City's relief rolls get $1.31 a day, broken down as follows: 65¢ for food, 21¢ for clothes, 22¢ for rent, 23¢ for other needs. Well, the upshot of it all was that the families were removed from their hotel rooms with maid service and radio, but at first, the press showed little interest in finding out where they'd gone beyond the bare statement that they'd been moved. Albert Deutsch of *PM* followed through, though. He learned that the families had been moved to condemned tenements and to the city's two municipal lodging houses. Perhaps prophetically, the *Times* had printed a story about how people live in these lodging houses—printed it at the height of the furor. Its reporter quoted Joseph Mannix, the director, as saying, "People are not supposed to stay here long. We take care of the homeless, but this place isn't a substitute for a permanent home."

The pictures accompanying Mr. Deutsch's article make that remark quite an example of understatement. To go back for a moment to those interesting circumstances under which the story got started. In his *Mirror* column one day, Walter Winchell addressed an aside to Mayor O'Dwyer, which read, "Do you know who is behind the current exposé to embarrass the city administration? Is he the jurist who asked you to get his wife a city job?" Next day, the *Mirror* itself told a little more in its news columns—it said that most of the relief cases involved in the hotel story had appeared before Justice James V. Mulholland in domestic relations court, because children and domestic difficulties were involved. The *Mirror* story went on to say that last fall Mayor O'Dwyer had refused to appoint Justice Mulholland's wife to the Board of Education. But it still wasn't plain how the *World-Telegram* had been first with the stories. *PM* said that a *Telegram* reporter, Walter MacDonald, is a friend of Justice Mulholland, and since reporters are not permitted to be present at proceedings in Children's Court, the inference is that Justice Mulholland gave his friend Reporter MacDonald a scoop. We've been trying to confirm this, but Mr.

MacDonald is out of town, according to the *Telegram*'s city desk, and can't be reached. Justice Mulholland is also unavailable for comment, but his wife said she was pretty sure he wouldn't want to say anything. The *Sun* said its information came from letters and telephone calls from employees of the Department of Welfare, but no names are used in its published accounts, naturally.

As the story dragged on, some other journalistic curiosities were produced. For instance, a number of private welfare agencies came to the defense of the Welfare Department, but this fact was ignored by the *Journal*, the *Telegram*, the *News*, and the *Mirror*. The *Times*, *Tribune*, and *Sun* gave it little prominence, and only the *Post* and *PM* thought it worthy of extensive treatment. Also, when Commissioner Rhatigan went on the air with his defense, the *News* and *Mirror* ignored it entirely. Of course, it's possible that the story appeared in one or two editions and was then dropped out, but it seems hardly likely that in a case of such continuing interest as the hotel relief story that this would have occurred. Mr. Rhatigan took the hide off the newspapers which had whooped up the story. He referred to two New York evening newspapers—NOT by name—and asked bitterly about the campaign they seemed to think so worthy of the great traditions of Greeley and Pulitzer. The *Sun* replied that this was just the old precept that, in the absence of a case, the best tactics for the defense are to abuse the lawyer for the plaintiff. But the *Telegram* showed that you can make every knock a boost, if you try. In reporting his speech, the *Telegram*'s first paragraph said, in part, to quote it, "Welfare Commissioner Rhatigan declared that recent publicity on the high cost of relief had dramatically spotlighted the rising load of destitution in the city."

Another civic matter with which the press has concerned itself extensively the past week has been the transit situation—the dispute between the transport workers union and the city's Board of Transportation over a proposed schedule alteration. The result was a slowdown of service on the Independent subway line, a slowdown which later was or was not called off, depending on which newspaper you read. But the most interesting journalistic event of the affair was the performance of the *New York Daily News* in its editions of last Thursday. In the first edition, the *News* printed a story on page 3, quoting William Jerome Daly, secretary of the Board of Transportation, as saying that if the board obtained proof of a deliberate slowdown in subway service, eight hundred motormen, conductors, and platform men responsible for the slowdown might be fired under the recently enacted state law which bans strikes by public employees. The story was written by William Price and Jack Turcott, and along with the account, a picture of Mr. Daly was printed. Mr. Daly saw this first edition—it appears on the streets between eight and nine o'clock in the evening—and Mr. Daly got cross. He called the *News* and demanded a withdrawal of the story and of his picture. The point being, he had never made any statement such as the *News* had attributed to him. So presumably, various things happened in the city room of the *New York Daily News*, and we next see the three-star edition of the paper, which is published several hours later. The page-one headline is the same, "800 Quill men may lose jobs; board acts to prove slowdown plot," but there is a difference in the story on page 3. Mr. Daly's name has disappeared; his picture has vanished, and in its place is one of Representative Thomas of New Jersey hunting Reds. Otherwise, the *News*'s story is the same; the only difference is that an unidentified board official is quoted as saying what the *News* had earlier attributed to Mr. Daly. This board official—NOT named—is pretty hard to locate and seems to be crossing himself up; the *Times* and *Mirror* of the same day quote him as denying that *any* firings were contemplated.

And now we come to a real journalistic mystery: *PM* and the *Daily Worker* also printed the statement attributed to Mr. Daly by the *News*, but where they got the story seems difficult to find out. *PM* said it came from the Associated Press, which disclaims all knowledge of it, so the suspicion must remain that *PM* lifted its story from the early edition of the *News* and, since its final edition goes to press much earlier, had no chance to change it. We've called the *Daily Worker* four times about their piece, but so far, they haven't told us where it came from.

One story of high finance and journalism that has been ignored by most of the press is the announcement that Winston Churchill's memoirs will be published serially in America in the *New York Times* and *Life* magazine for an amount of money said by the *Times* to be in excess of one million dollars. That million is only for the American rights; Mr. Churchill's memoirs will also appear in England, Australia, and South Africa and will later be republished in book form to the extent of five volumes, all of which will make Mr. Churchill one of the highest-paid writers of his time.

And the trade paper of journalism, *Editor & Publisher*, tells a story which shows the former prime minister to be a pretty sharp businessman as well as a prolific writer. Mr. Churchill, the story says, would contract to write an article of certain length but demand proofs to correct. When he returned those proofs, the corrections would make his article somewhat longer, and a bill for the extra wordage would be sent to the publisher. Less-prominent toilers in the vineyards of journalism seldom are able to be so exacting, but some of them turn in some fine work for a lot less money. Among them should be mentioned Robert S. Bird of the *Herald Tribune*. Mr. Bird was sent by his newspaper to report the recent lynch trial at Greenville, South Carolina, and the CBS newsroom staff is in general agreement that Mr. Bird's dispatches were the best which appeared in the New York press. Mr. Bird did a particularly excellent job of reporting the reactions of the community to the national attention which the story of the trial commanded.

We all liked, too, Billy Rose's column in *PM* last Tuesday—a short story, really, about a war correspondent trying to convert from war to peace and the contrast between his former glamorous status as a big shot and his attempt to write an acceptable story about the auto show.

Most of us didn't like a comment by Westbrook Pegler in the *Journal-American* Thursday. In the course of his article, Mr. Pegler referred to Sidney Hillman and David Dubinsky, the labor leaders, with a slur on their use of the English language—"dialect unioneers," he called them. Mr. Pegler's column was a sentimental recall of the days when newspaper men were figures of greater stature than they are today, which could be: they probably wouldn't find it amusing to comment on an immigrant's accent.

One of the things which most concerns anyone in the business of reporting news is accuracy; the conscientious reporter's main concern is that names are correct and facts straight. Naturally, that goes for broadcast as well as written news. This comes to mind because of the story of Clem McCarthy, who broadcast the Belmont Stakes for CBS earlier this afternoon. The story of Clem at the Preakness is pretty well known—how he inadvertently announced the wrong horse as the winner. But there's an amusing sequel to the story which puts an odd twist on it. Incidentally, Clem's colleagues among the sportswriters were most generous about his fumble, fully aware of the difficulty of identifying horses and jockeys half a mile away and trying to tell the world about it at the same time. Discussing it later, in his radio column in the *Times,* Jack Gould wrote that the error would have no ill effects on Clem's radio career, that he would report the Belmont Stakes for CBS on May 31—which Clem did correctly, we are happy to say. The only thing was that Mr. Gould had one of those lapses too; he said the error occurred at the Kentucky Derby. Writing and talking news are hazardous occupations indeed, but Clem and Mr. Gould would now appear to have finished in a dead heat, so far as slips of tongue and typewriter are concerned.

## June 14, 1947

In a half-dozen programs, Hollenbeck criticized discriminatory coverage by the press. He was influenced by Margaret "Peg" Halsey, a next-door neighbor and close friend, who wrote *Color Blind: A White Woman Looks at the Negro* (1946). In fighting discrimination, Halsey wrote, "The main thing is to select something that is in line with your own personality and something that falls within the framework of your life."[1] Hollenbeck resigned from his racially discriminatory fraternity, Phi Kappa Psi. He squelched racist comments by CBS associates. He devoted *CBS Views the Press* broadcasts to applauding exemplary reporting. He suggested that Ray Sprigle, a white reporter who darkly tanned his skin and traveled four thousand miles though the Deep South as a black man, deserved a second Pulitzer Prize for his twenty-one-part series, "In the Land of Jim Crow." Hollenbeck also celebrated a prize-winning series by the *New York Post*'s Ted Poston, said to be the only black reporter working at a New York metropolitan daily. And, as this broadcast indicates, Hollenbeck blasted Jim Crow journalism.

JIM CROW IS A JOURNALIST, as we learn from reading the daily press. Jim Crow is a journalist, not only in the section of our country where the law gives him full sanction but right here in New York City, where it does NOT. Jim Crow has one drinking fountain for whites, another for Negroes, the front of the bus for whites, the rear for Negroes. It also has one code of ethics for writing about white people and another for Negro people. During the past week we've had a good opportunity to note some examples of Jim Crowism in the daily newspapers, but before we comment on them, a little background may be helpful.

1. Margaret Halsey, *Color Blind: A White Woman Looks at the Negro* (New York: Simon and Schuster, 1946), 150.

June 14, 1947

About ten years ago, the National Association for the Advancement of Colored People asked the press associations and the major newspapers of the nation to consider for possible adoption an order in force on the *New York Post*: that color or race shall NOT be used in describing anyone connected with a crime unless color or race is an essential part of the story. Typical of many replies was that received from the *New York Herald Tribune* which read, and I quote it: "It is our policy now in the treatment of news not to emphasize the color or race of a man involved in a crime. All our editors know this, and our reporters and copyreaders. Color and race are put into our stories only when essential. We endeavor to enforce this policy at all times."

Almost all the editors who replied made the reservation that when designation of race or color seemed essential to clarity, they would then designate race or color. One thing that NAACP request did stop pretty largely was the designation of race or color in headlines. It also helped a lot to reduce racial discrimination in news stories themselves, but it hasn't helped enough, as our examination of some evidence shows now. Last Monday morning, page 3 of the *Daily News* was quite a spectacle. All but six lines of type were devoted to crime news and pictures.

Most prominent on this page was the story of the sixty-nine-year-old Brooklyn minister who rescued his wife from an attacker, who was later quickly caught by the police. The opening paragraph of the *Daily News* story, in heavy type, identified the accused man as a Negro—not by a name, which he has as we all have, but simply by his color. The same identification was used three more times in the body of the story; apparently the writers and editors who worked on this story felt it was essential to clarity to repeat this point.

A similar performance was turned in by the *Journal-American*, which used the word "Negro" three times. The *Mirror* used it once, in the opening paragraph; so did the *Sun*. In the *Times* and *Herald Tribune*, the identification was made once, well down in their stories, and the *Tribune* used it only on direct quotation from the pastor.

To their credit, the *World-Telegram*, the *Post*, and *PM* did not once describe the accused attacker in terms of his color. The point made by the NAACP in its letter to newspaper editors was that repeated usage of color designation had aroused in the public mind a belief that the Negro is more addicted to crime than any other group, and to quote the letter, "a belief which impartial studies have revealed is not the case."

It seems scarcely necessary to point out that other groups and nationalities aren't marked for specific mention, and as the NAACP asks, quote, "Is it too much to ask that the single exception which not all, but many, newspapers make of singling out Negroes for designation in headlines and text of crime stories be done away with?"

That letter was written ten years ago. It (and perhaps the consciences of editors) have succeeded in getting most of the Jim Crowism out of the headlines, but there are still some jobs to be done. That fact is all too apparent in an example or two of the reporting turned in by some of the press associations, as well. Early this month, a tornado struck down South, and a number of people were killed. I quote now the opening sentence of an Associated Press dispatch of June 3, under a Pine Bluff, Arkansas, dateline: "A Negro whose automobile was plucked from the highway and flung into a cotton field by Sunday's tornado died today of his injuries, bringing the official death toll of the storm to thirty-five." That man who was killed by the storm had a name, as we all do, and the Associated Press is usually most reliable about getting names. In this case, the victim's color alone seemed to be enough identification.

Or another Associated Press dispatch of a few days earlier, from Raleigh, North Carolina, in which Godwin Bush, who escaped from a lynch mob, was described as "almost illiterate." Perhaps he hadn't been given the same opportunities for education as the Associated Press reporter. Incidentally, this reference to the young man's illiteracy was printed in both the *Times* and *Herald Tribune*, which are usually more scrupulous about such things. The fact of Godwin Bush's literacy was no more pertinent to the story than would have been the fact of his left-handedness, if he had been left-handed. As used, it was simply a slur. But that would appear to have been a case of momentary forgetfulness on the copy desk; both the *Times* and *Herald Tribune* are to be commended for their general policy on race relations. George Streator of the *Times*, for instance, has been going around the country studying the problem in terms of housing and employment.

The *Tribune* recently had an excellent series of articles by Robert J. Donovan on the Negro struggle for education in Texas. The *Post*, *PM*, and the *Daily Worker* also deal extensively with stories of this type, but they confine their reports mostly to the New York area. When our CBS newsroom staff talked over this matter of Jim Crow in journalism, one member asked, "But if you leave out the color identification in a crime story, aren't you guilty of suppressing legitimate news?" The answer to that one was, "Are other persons so identified? White? Anglo-Saxon? Jewish, Danish, French, whatever? Not so you could notice it."

It was interesting this week to note the performance of the newspapers in their treatment of the CIO rally calling for a veto of the Taft-Hartley labor bill. The preliminary story in the *World-Telegram* on the day of the rally turned up an example of an extremely interesting journalistic device. One sentence read as follows, and I quote it: "Reports that fines would be imposed on any member not attending the rally were scoffed at by CIO spokesmen." Okay, reports by whom? It is certainly common practice in journalism to cite these rather vague reports; sometimes, where sources of information cannot be quoted, the practice is justified, if used with care and integrity. But when, as in this case, a report is set up like a straw man—no hint of a source given—only to be knocked down by a denial, the practice is something else again. The point the *World-Telegram* apparently wanted to make remained in the reader's mind: it had been reported that union members who stayed away from the rally would be fined.

The denial got lost in the shuffle, even though that denial was repeated by CIO officials. It might as well have been a report that the paraders were going to march backward that was denied so far as any facts were concerned. Reports of the attendance at the rally also got a reportorial kicking around: Joseph Curran of the CIO, who superintended arrangements for the parade, was quoted by the *Daily News* as estimating that anywhere from 70,000 to 115,000 were in the line of march. The United Press wire, which serves radio stations, that evening guessed 140,000, and that's the figure WCBS used to inform its listeners. Much later, the United Press cut the figure to 60,000. That was the estimate by police, which is usually taken as official, although in this case, maybe Mayor O'Dwyer might have been happier if his police guessers hadn't trimmed it so sharply; the mayor was a prime mover in the rally and anxious for it to be a success. But no matter how many people were involved in it, there wasn't a line about the rally in next morning's *Mirror*, and somebody on the *News* betrayed a faulty ear for music when, in the paper's first edition, he wrote that there was sporadic singing of the "Communist Internationale." In later editions of the paper the title was changed to "Solidarity Forever," which is a good old American union song.

Readers of the *Journal-American* undoubtedly were impressed the other day by a full-page picture story—impressed first of all, perhaps, because the picture story was printed sideways on the page. If they turned the page around to study it, they saw pictures of two New York housing developments, one public, the other private.

The private job—Stuyvesant Town—was pretty well along, but the public one was still in the foundation stage. The headline accompanying the pictures pointed out that the private project had been started in 1945—tenants will move in soon, it said. The public project was started in 1943—work barely started. Bureaucratic fumbling, it went on—here were two spectacular examples of private enterprise versus socialistic government planning. We collected a few facts on this matter, which are as follows: Excavation work on the private development began seven months before it did on the public one, and the latter will be ready for occupancy by November. Demolition, it is true, had been done on the government project in 1943, but the excavation for the private job had beat the government one by seven months. Another point the *Journal-American* didn't mention was that another public housing development—Eliot Houses—was started at the same time Stuyvesant Town was, and tenants are already living in Eliot Houses. Whatever the virtues of the arguments over public and private housing are, in these days when all kinds of housing are needed, it might not be a bad idea to report the complete facts on all efforts to relieve the shortage before drawing conclusions.

Better reporting was done through the week by Walter Arm of the *Herald Tribune* and Leon Edel of *PM*—both of them turned in good jobs of journalism on the Douglas Chandler treason trial in Boston. We liked Albion Ross's dispatches in the *Times,* analyzing the political situation in Austria, and, closer to home, Joseph Mackey's excellent story in the *Sun* on how some youthful gangs in New York got together and formed an organization patterned after the United Nations.

We liked Murray Robinson's series of articles in the *Telegram*—well-written and not-too-technical stories about how athletes get in condition after the winter layoff. Interesting and informative even to nonreaders of the sports pages. Mr. Robinson is one of the ablest members of an able staff on the *World-Telegram,* which, in the opinion of our news staff, does the best job in town with what are called feature stories—out-of-the-ordinary yarns about people, animals, or whatnot. They can make even the weather forecast interesting, and a weather forecast is usually difficult to lift out of the routine. There's Arpad, for instance.

Arpad is the *World-Telegram*'s bumptious, foppish weathercock, which has become well known to New Yorkers over a ten-year period. Three days a week there's a front-page cartoon of Arpad cutting some foolish dido or other and, along with it, a seemingly pointless little story, which eventually ends up with the weather prediction for the day. Close followers of Arpad know that cartoonist Bill Pause has been drawing the rooster for ten years, starting him out as a simple weather vane, with no interest in the fancy clothes Arpad has now. But few know much about the stories which accompany the drawings. They were started by H. Allen Smith, who gave the rooster his name, wrote the zany yarns for awhile, and then went on to become low man on a totem pole, and to other literary achievements. In the ten years Arpad has been assisting with the weather predictions, he has had eleven Boswells, the present ones being Mr. Robinson and Fred Cook. Mr. Robinson writes the stories twice a week, Mr. Cook does them once. Incidentally, the question of which came first, chicken or egg, has an answer in Arpad. Bill Pause does the drawings first, then the writers scramble their literary omelets later.

The *World-Telegram* has also been printing a very informative series of articles on conditions in New York City schools. The *Telegram* articles are being done by Walter MacDonald and Norton Mockridge, two of the newspaper's specialists in stories of this type involving investigation. Mr. MacDonald will be remembered as the author of the series of articles on "luxury relief," a series discussed earlier on this program. Mr. MacDonald has also been writing about relief again, but he has taken a new tack. When the state began its investigation into the administration of New York City relief, Mr. MacDonald pointed out that in anticipation of the hearings, the city's Department of Welfare has clamped down on "special services" to clients to the point where some needy and worthy cases are suffering hardship. Evidently, so far as the *Telegram* is concerned, it's a case of darned if you do and darned if you don't.

But the most surprising change of pace in the relief story has been shown in the articles by William Wyer of the *Sun.* The stories by Mr. Wyer weren't far behind those of Mr. MacDonald in the original hullabaloo over so-called deluxe relief. In some respects his stories even went the *World-Telegram* one or two better. But this week there appeared in the *Sun* a series of articles by Mr. Wyer on the general subject of New York City relief—a thorough, carefully documented history of the matter since 1930. The series of four articles may well be preserved for their objective tone and factual slant. It does seem unusual that the same Mr. Wyer could have written them and the deluxe stories, too. One is forced to wonder that if he'd written the present series first, he might have handled the others in quite a different way.

In checking the newspapers this week, we almost missed an extremely interesting item in the *Sun.* Away back on page 21 of Wednesday's issue, there was a paragraph at the end of a story which said the state board making its investigation into the city relief situation would have a report ready by June 24. The story ended with this paragraph, and I quote it: "At the same time, it was announced that the Welfare Department was forced to place four other families, totaling sixteen persons, in hotel rooms because of the housing shortage."

Anybody want to get excited?

## July 12, 1947

The Communist threat to the United States was not make-believe. While there were American Communists who were idealistic radical populists, there also were American Communists who were committed to the totalitarian Soviet Union. Many media adopted a brand of anti-Communism that consistently overstated the impact of Communism inside the United States and smeared critics who questioned their overstatements, labeling them Communist sympathizers or dupes. This broadcast, which criticized a banner-headline story in the *New York Sun* titled "Secret A bomb files are stolen from Oak Ridge," incensed the *Sun*'s management. The paper demanded time on the next program for rebuttal. The *Sun*'s rebuttal, delivered by Col. Gilbert T. Hodges, chairman of the *Sun*'s executive committee, ended with a spoonful of innuendo. Hodges pointed out that Hollenbeck was an alumnus of the newspaper *PM* and went on, "Far be it from me to imply that the *PM* newspaper has any Socialistic or Communistic leanings." Then Hodges said Hollenbeck, whose "affection for *PM* continues strong," was a liberal who followed "the party line which such liberals invariably pursue," implying the party line that Hollenbeck followed was the line of the Communists.[1]

IN THE *NEW YORK SUN* of September 21, 1897, there appeared an editorial which has probably been reprinted as widely as any editorial ever written. An eight-year-old girl had been told by some of her friends that there was no Santa Claus, and she was writing to the editor of the *Sun* to get the facts. She wrote, "Papa says, 'If you see it in the *Sun*, it's so.'" A *Sun* writer named Francis P. Church made himself immortal in journalism with his editorial replying to the little girl. He wrote that her little friends were wrong—that

1. *CBS Views the Press*, July 19, 1947, transcript, 8.

they had been affected by the skepticism of a skeptical age. She might get her papa to hire men to watch in all the chimneys on Christmas Eve to catch Santa Claus, but even if they didn't see him coming down, that wouldn't prove anything. Nobody sees Santa Claus, but that's no sign there isn't a Santa Claus. It was a beautiful job, that editorial, and it will be long remembered and referred to. Readers of the *Sun* with long memories might have been reminded of it in a somewhat different connection last Wednesday; or perhaps their papas, too, had at one time told them that if they saw it in the *Sun*, it was so.

The 314,000 readers of the *Sun* picked up their newspapers that day, and in three banner lines of heavy type they read, "Secret A bomb files are stolen from Oak Ridge." Under the signature of Edward Nellor, of the *Sun*'s Washington staff, the story went on to say that unknown agents, working from within the atomic-energy plant at Oak Ridge, Tennessee, have stolen several files of highly secret data on the atomic bomb. No names, no dates were given, and very few details for such an important story, but it was plainly hinted that it was a Communist job. As might have been expected, the story caused a sensation and was taken straight to the White House, where all knowledge of it was disclaimed. The FBI had no immediate comment. The security officer at the Oak Ridge plant told the United Press he knew of no basis whatever for the story. Then Senator Hickenlooper of Iowa, who is chairman of the joint congressional committee on atomic energy, came forth with an explanation. On the Senate floor, he said that in March 1946 there had been a theft of some atomic-energy data from the plant at Los Alamos—that the FBI had caught the culprits, who turned out to be two army sergeants employed on the project at the time. Senator Hickenlooper said the FBI had told his committee the sergeants had taken the data simply as an interesting memento of their jobs. No prosecution was made at the time, but now there may be, although that is still unsettled.

In a later statement, Senator Hickenlooper repeated his denial of the *Sun*'s story; he said the theft by the army sergeants was the only case of the disappearance of any important material of any kind that we know of, and he added that this statement specifically covered the Oak Ridge plant. He concluded, and I quote him, "I am assured on the highest possible authority, and I know I can say with certainty, that there are no missing materials of any substantial importance at all from Oak Ridge or any other installations." President Truman had been asked about it, and he said he thought Senator Hickenlooper had covered the points pretty thoroughly.

With this in mind, we can consider the basis in fact for this alarming story in the *Sun*. It was written so positively as to reassure papa that if you see it in the *Sun*, it's so, even though it was denied with the skepticism of those who would have it that there is no Santa Claus. The first to be asked, naturally, was the man who wrote the story, Edward Nellor. Mr. Nellor has been with the *Sun* about six years, having formerly worked on a newspaper in the Northwest. He first worked in the New York office of the *Sun* and was then transferred to Washington, where, according to Keats Speed, executive editor of the *Sun*, he has a splendid record. If you want to know what he looks like, you can probably see him at a movie; Pathe newsreel did an interview with him.

To CBS, Mr. Nellor said he was convinced of his story's accuracy, and he'd stand by it. He did, too, as readers will recall: Senator Hickenlooper's explanation was printed in the *Sun* as the account of "another" theft of atomic-energy data, although in his speech on the Senate floor referring to the story, Senator Hickenlooper said there were a number of apparent conjectures in it, perhaps based on suspicion, perhaps based upon guess. He said he felt the story might bring a wrong connotation in so far as security is concerned.

In stories of this type, involving information obtained from unstated but confidential sources, reporters are usually not willing to say very much about where they got their facts; it is their recognized right and duty to protect their sources of information if they feel obliged to. But Mr. Nellor was willing to go farther than most in filling in the background of the story. He said the tip on it had come from what he described as a frightened assistant to the congressional committee—the same committee headed by Senator Hickenlooper. This assistant, Mr. Nellor said, had told him he reflected the anxiety of some members of the committee—not identified—but from two of these members, Mr. Nellor says, he got his story. And he had other help he was willing to identify: Representative J. Parnell Thomas of New Jersey, Mr. Nellor says, gave him some information, although Representative Thomas is not a member of the congressional Atomic Energy Committee; he heads the House Un-American Activities Committee.

And that brings up another point: before Senator Hickenlooper had made his official denial of the *Sun*'s story, Representative Thomas was out with a statement. It was even incorporated in the *Sun*'s first story. He said the *Sun*'s story came as no surprise to him. Representative Thomas added that Mr. Nellor's story offered new justification for military control of atomic energy, and that brings up another curious point: the timing of the *Sun* article. Just the day before it appeared, the congressional Atomic Energy Committee had met to consider five bills which would abolish the present civilian commission headed by David Lilienthal. One of the measures would transfer all atomic projects and properties to the War Department. The second paragraph of Mr. Nellor's story said the disclosure—and I'm quoting—"the disclosure is expected to blast the nation's atomic-energy setup into a total reorganization."

Thus the story appeared when it might have vitally affected pending legislation. The New Jersey representative has been a leader in asking military control of atomic energy. Now as to the way the rest of the New York press reacted to the *Sun* story: The *Post*, the *Daily Worker*, and *PM* followed the predictable course of razzing it. It was I. F. Stone in *PM* who was quick to point out the timing of the story, and James A. Wechsler in the *Post* wrote, "It appeared that the story reportedly planted by supporters of military control had blown up in their faces after Senator Hickenlooper's statement." The *Journal* followed the *Sun*, along with trimmings by its cartoonist, Burris Jenkins Jr., who pictured Uncle Sam in bed, menaced by what were labeled "deadly, Communistic-controlled A-bomb employees" coming through a broken screen.

Finally, statements by two editors regarding the *Sun* story are of interest. The first is by Keats Speed, executive editor of the *Sun*, who said, "We know the story is true. We knew it was true before we printed it, and the *Sun* will stick by the story from beginning to end." And then this comment in Thursday's *Herald Tribune* in the form of an editorial—a rare one for the *Tribune*, which doesn't often criticize another paper. The editorial read as follows, in part: "Those who write and speak about the atom are not expected to imprison themselves in silence; but it does not appear unreasonable to ask that the gravity of the situation imbue them with a sense of responsibility. The report yesterday alleging serious breaches in atomic security did not live up to this standard. . . . Unless those who inspired it are in possession of information denied to Senator Hickenlooper . . . and to the security officer at Oak Ridge, it was in all important respects untrue."

The *Herald Tribune* editorial also pointed out that the atom bomb, or anything directly connected with it, is America's exposed nerve. It added, "An even-minded America is essential if the nations of the world are to reach an agreement that will convert atomic energy from a menace to a promise." The *Sun*'s implication that Russia was involved in the supposed Oak Ridge case doesn't read like even-minded America; the exposed nerve of America got quite a rubbing by the *Sun*'s story. On the authority of the president of the United States, the chairman of the congressional Atomic Energy Committee, and the security officer at Oak Ridge, the *Sun*'s story had no basis in fact. If we accept these authorities, the question must then arise, what purpose was served by it except to rub nerves already raw, to worsen relations with Russia, already bad enough.

The *Times* wrote an epitaph to lay to rest the Oak Ridge ghost summoned up by the *Sun*. A *Times* editorial said, "We do not believe the atomic secret is something that can be written down in a page or two, like a recipe for corn bread . . . and . . . that it will never be carried overseas in the heel of a shoe. The atom is in good hands. No facts thus far revealed warrant hysteria."

The international nerve-rubbing even got into the story of the flying saucers, which first had America wondering, worrying, and finally laughing. At the height of the excitement, one read in the *Journal-American* that somebody had written a letter to the *Los Angeles Examiner* describing Russian supersonic atom-powered planes as resembling the flying saucers, and the story went on to say that a top-flight atomic scientist, not identified, had assured the *Examiner* that the letter wasn't all nonsense.

But wonderful nonsense was what the flying-saucer story turned into pretty soon, and although the things were seen in Technicolor, it became difficult to see them as entirely Red. Some very fine stories were turned in about the flying saucers, and among the best was one in the *Sun* on Tuesday. It was a mock-scientific, kidding account of the whole affair, with a solemn discussion of whether the saucers might really be another sort of crockery. The writer explained that a saucer is always, well, saucer-shaped, whereas plates and dishes are plate-ish and dish-ish, respectively. Inquiry of the *Sun*'s city desk as to who had written this refreshing piece brought the answer that the paper would prefer to have it known that it was done only by a member of the staff, so recognition must go to the invisible man. And apparently the desk didn't think so much of it at that. In later editions that same day, the story was replaced by something about what Admiral Blandy thought of the flying disks—not half so entertaining and about as important as what airplane inventor Orville Wright had to say about the saucers:

that the whole thing was simply a government campaign to get put into another war by stirring up our fears. That one was ignored by most of the newspapers, but the *Daily Worker* gave it prominence. The saucer story finally wound up in the advertising columns, an especially clever one being a savings bank's announcement that the disks are really the pennies, nickels, dimes, and so on which slip through our fingers. And a press agent took it over, inevitably; from the Earle Associates Inc. came the announcement that a flying-saucer dress has been created.

A United Nations delegate from Canada read the *Sun*'s atomic-theft story and the bank's advertisement about flying disks and said, "What a country!" He might have made it even stronger if he were a reader of some of our comic strips.

In federal court in Newark last month, Judge Thomas F. Meaney heard a case which called for a ruling on the question of whether a comic supplement is part of a newspaper; a technicality concerning their transportation by a trucking company was at issue. In his decision, Judge Meaney said, "The present-day newspaper, in addition to carrying items of general news interest, contains enormous quantities of advertising, political comment, chess problems, crossword puzzles, and what are called (often with lamentable inaccuracy) comics."

It doesn't require a federal court decision to determine how dear to the hearts of the newspaper-reading public are the imaginary creatures of the comic strip. That was demonstrated more than a quarter of a century ago when a character named Skeezix was born to become a member of the cast of *Gasoline Alley*; readers swamped Skeezix with gifts and good wishes. Comics have changed into some rather baffling forms since Skeezix was born, but the public's devotion to the characters in them hasn't altered a bit. That has been demonstrated again in the reaction to a comic strip blessed event: the birth of a golden-haired girl named Sparkles to Mr. and Mrs. B. O. Plenty, Mrs. Plenty's other name being Gravel Gertie. In the *Dick Tracy* strip, they make about the world's most repellent couple.

But for all their unlovely looks, B. O. Plenty and Gravel Gertie have a host of friends; the syndicate which distributes the *Dick Tracy* feature to three hundred newspapers, including the *Daily News,* is resting up from a flurry of work following Sparkles's birth May 30. Both syndicate offices in Chicago and New York were swamped with telephone calls. There were countless congratulatory cards—or so enthusiastic syndicate workers said—and many gifts: flowers from persons not averse to a little publicity themselves, and there were hand-knitted booties, sweaters, rattles, high-chair pads, a diaper bag, a live turtle no handsomer than B. O. Plenty himself, a whiskey bottle with nipple attached, a phony check for a thousand dollars, and one dollar in cash.

As outlandish as some of the so-called comics are these days, it is perhaps just as well that they are in the hands of the artists and continuity writers who are doing them because among the many names suggested by readers for Miss Plenty were Disinfectant and Muddy Mamie. Earl Carroll's press agent reads *Dick Tracy,* too; among the congratulatory telegrams was one signed by Mr. Carroll offering Miss Sparkle a contract for his *Vanities* of 1965. The question this response raises is what becomes of all the hodge-podge of messages and gifts received by the syndicate. All the messages are answered—you've got to keep the readers happy—and the gifts are sorted out by the artist, in this case Chester Gould, who has a studio in Woodstock, Illinois. The more unusual ones he keeps as trophies—testimony that the comic page is one of the most important parts of a newspaper.

But in the welter of flying-saucer stories lately, the news pages began to give the comics some competition for fantasy, and Dick Tracy himself got involved in the atomic-secret theft story: the *Sun* made the assertion that congressmen are just now recovering from the discovery that the entire approach of atomic security smacked of Dick Tracy. Well, on the comic page at least, Dick Tracy is infallible; he's never suspected of error.

## November 1, 1947

In 1947 the House Committee on Un-American Activities (HUAC) declared that Hollywood moviemakers were producing films that glorified the Communist system. The committee held closed-session hearings in Los Angeles in May, then open sessions in Washington in October and November. "Are you now or were you ever a Communist?" the committee asked witnesses. Twenty-four witnesses "friendly" to the committee, including actor Ronald Reagan, president of the Screen Actors Guild, testified. Eleven "unfriendly" witnesses—German dramatist Bertolt Brecht, who immediately left the country after testifying, and ten writers and directors, the "Hollywood Ten"—also appeared before the committee. Charged with contempt of Congress for refusing to cooperate, the Ten received jail sentences of six to twelve months each and were blacklisted, kept from working in Hollywood for years. Lauren Bacall, Humphrey Bogart, and other Hollywood celebrities formed the Committee for the First Amendment, which traveled to Washington to protest the HUAC hearings. Don Hollenbeck's *CBS Views the Press* used the extraordinary press coverage of the HUAC hearings to make an important point: News is manufactured—"what you make it"—not just a report of recent events. Depending on the newspaper doing the manufacturing, the coverage of the HUAC was evenhanded (the *Times* and *Herald Tribune*), critical of the committee (the *Post* and *PM*), or supportive of it (the *Journal-American*, *World-Telegram*, *Sun*, *News*, and *Mirror*).

ONE OF NOAH WEBSTER'S early definitions of "news" is this: "a report of a recent event; information about something before unknown; fresh tidings, recent intelligence." That definition served pretty adequately in the early days of newspapers, when about all they could do was to report on a recent event, give information about something before unknown, bring fresh tidings and recent intelligence—no matter if the tidings and intelligence were a long way behind the event. But newspapers altered, and so did the definition of "news." A later entry in Webster defines it thus: "matter adapted to gaining the interest of newspaper readers." The editors of the dictionary had perhaps become a little confused as to exactly what news is and had taken the safe course of saying, in effect, "news is what you make it." You can adapt matter to gain the interest of newspaper readers. A more cynical and realistic definition than the earlier one in the light of the way newspapers operate today—and examination of one particular story and its treatment by the press during the last two weeks certainly proves that news is what you make it.

The story is that of the proceedings at the investigation into Communist activity in Hollywood by the House Committee on Un-American Activities—how the newspapers treated it and why they approached it from one point of view or another. For one thing, they all treated it to lavish amounts of space; any story involving the names of a lot of movie people is going to command respectful attention on the part of editors, who realize the news value of the subject. But that can take a curious twist, too, as we'll see, because there is more to this story than just a lot of glamorous movie folk going to Washington. There are matters involved that are far more serious to all of us: the extent of the Communist threat to the nation and the right of individuals to hold certain political beliefs and to express them. Movie stars, writers, and directors alone didn't make the story a big one; these people merely provided a dramatic manner of presenting the two main questions: the extent of the Communist threat to the nation and the right of individuals to hold in privacy their political beliefs.

We have read lots of type and looked at lots of pictures about this hearing. And incidentally, Frank Scully of *Variety* made our favorite comment about the camera coverage when he wrote, "What the photographers have done to the glamour boys via their candid cameras is terrifying." Poor Cooper, poor Taylor, poor Wood, poor Menjou, poor Yorick. It was a shock to see them looking like alien gargoyles. And Mr. Scully went on to suggest that Hollywood's own cameramen and makeup artists ought to ask for salary increases commensurate with the illusions they produce. *Time* magazine seemed to go out of its way to select the most grotesque photos of anti-Communist witnesses, and its story was very sardonic about the whole affair.

But to get back to the columns of type: sometimes they have seemed as fuzzy and grotesque as the pictures, and we're going to try today to get them into some sort of focus. Readers of just one or two newspapers will get just one or two specific notions of the movie hearing, depending upon the way those one or two newspapers are presenting it to them. This can be said at the outset: readers of the *New York Times* and the *New York Herald Tribune* have consistently received the fairest, most unbiased account of a sometimes confusing and befuddled performance. Both newspapers had come out editorially against the committee's procedure in conducting the investigation, but in their news columns, both were careful to present both sides of the controversy in terms of what actually happened at the hearing. Their news stories led off with the actual testimony, which was proper, and then went on to present statements opposing the committee—statements by lawyers and by groups of other interested parties. If it were a toss-up, our vote for the best job would go to Carl Levin of the *Herald Tribune.*

The *Times* and *Tribune* both used the traditional newspaper treatment of "first things first," even though those opposed to the practices of the committee have objected that the treatment gives a lop-sided picture of the situation. They say more prominence has been given the accusations against alleged Communists or Communist sympathizers than has been given those who challenged the committee; most of those challenges, of course, are not a part of the record. *PM* and the *Post* have given prominence to the proceedings in the committee room itself, but equal or more prominent—by headlines, display, and so forth—has been their presentation of the opposition's case.

The rest of the newspapers—the *Journal-American, World-Telegram, Sun, News,* and *Mirror*—have been frankly procommittee in their news columns and in their editorials and haven't bothered to waste much ink or space on the opposition. That showed up very clearly when the airplane-load of Hollywood stars made a cross-country trip to Washington to register their protest at the committee's practices—or they tried to register one, anyway. There had been big movie names testifying on the committee's side; the procommittee papers had given them their due share of attention and had faithfully and fully reported what they said. But there were—from the box-office standpoint at any rate—some equally big names in that plane-load of stars: Humphrey Bogart, Lauren Bacall, Danny Kaye, and others. In the *Times* and *Tribune,* they got fair play and better than an even break in *PM* and the *Post.* They didn't in the *Telegram,* which played them down, and they certainly didn't in the *Journal-American* story.

The headline about their trip said, "Probe to hear official data on film Reds"; this had nothing to do with the Bogart party, which was referred to in David Sentner's account as a propaganda group, ready to scream to high heaven. And in the same newspaper, Frank Conniff's piece read as follows: "Unless all signs and portents deceive, the splendid showing made by the representatives of the movie industry during the first week's hearing on Hollywood Communism will be marred very shortly by a crew of freeloading publicity hounds anxious to get their names in the paper at the expense of the film colony's name." They were all movie people—procommittee and concommittee alike—but to the *Journal-American,* one group made a splendid showing, another group was a crew of publicity hounds; but if they were, they failed to get an even break with the others.

But the most interesting journalistic development of the hearing was the constant promise we got in some quarters that we ain't seen nothin' yet—just wait until the big blow-off comes. It began with headlines in the *World-Telegram* and *Journal-American* such as these: "Charge Hollywood spy ring. Prober promises exposé of pipeline to Moscow." And in the story, this statement, quoting a committee spokesman: "We will show the existence of a Hollywood spy ring and a definite program of espionage." In the *Journal-American*, the following: "Evidence will be conclusive." In the *Mirror*: "Spokesman asserted testimony on espionage in Hollywood would be well-documented." In the *Sun* of last Monday, this: "Surprise witness predicted today to tie in Soviet with movie Reds. Chairman [J. Parnell] Thomas indicates new revelation will shock nation." Next day in the *World-Telegram*: "The proof will be there. Everybody will be convinced that there is a definite tie-up between Hollywood Communists and Soviet Russia." Same Tuesday, *Journal-American*: "A startling story of Soviet espionage operations involving the film industry." What were these headlines and phrases based on? Supposed inside information, but mostly they were spoon-fed to the reporters by Chairman Thomas of the committee, or that ever-present "spokesman." In many cases, Chairman Thomas was quoted directly as being just about to unload the big surprise, and last Thursday he held a news conference at which the Associated Press quoted him as saying the day's hearing would bring sensational evidence about atom-bomb espionage—a surprise witness has evidence to show certain movieland Reds were key figures in a plot to steal the secret of the bomb.

Perhaps there was a plot, perhaps some Hollywood figures had something to do with it, but so far, the story has not lived up to the advance billing given it by much of the press in the form of statements and promises and hints—blown up into big headlines. The *Herald Tribune* pointed out that the disclosure was not directly connected with the motion-picture industry or any of its alleged Communists. The *Times* said the connection with the motion-picture industry was little more than incidental. Neither the *Times* nor the *Tribune* had lent themselves to the hoo-la buildup some of the other papers had.

It is interesting to contrast the running story of the inquiry with another story of some importance made public last Wednesday. That was a report to the president of the United States by a committee on civil rights, appointed by him to determine the state of civil liberties in this country. Although the papers gave it some prominence, it didn't get anything like the prominence the Communist investigation did, of course, but one or two points in it are pertinent to this case. In passing, full marks to *PM* for printing the full text of the report in its weekend edition.

In discussing freedom of opinion, the committee rightly denounced Communism and Fascism and those who would foist either of them upon our people. It said that both often use the words and symbols of democracy to mask their totalitarian tactics and feel no obligation to come before the public openly and say who they are and what they really want.

But the committee went on to say that our national past offers us two great touchstones to resolve the dilemma of maintaining the right to free expression and yet protecting our democracy against its enemies. One was offered by Jefferson in his first inaugural: "If there be any among us who wish to dissolve the Union, or to change its republican form, let them stand undisturbed as monuments of the safety with which error of opinion may be tolerated where reason is left free to combat it." The second is the doctrine of clear and present danger, laid down by the late Supreme Court Justice Holmes. It says that no limitation of freedom of expression shall be made unless the words are used in such circumstances and are of such a nature as to create a clear and present danger that they will bring about the substantive evils that Congress has a right to prevent. The committee went on to say that it believed the present threat to freedom of opinion grows out of the failure of some public and private persons to apply those two standards at the same time, admitting that the "reason" upon which Jefferson relied to combat error is hampered by the successful efforts of some totalitarians to conceal their true nature.

The committee then went on to say that what it calls a state of near-hysteria about Communists now threatens to inhibit the freedom of genuine democrats—that if we fall back on hysteria and repression as our weapons against totalitarianism, we will defeat ourselves. Communists, the report said, want nothing more than to be lumped with freedom-loving non-Communists; it simply makes it easier for them to conceal their true nature and to allege that the term "Communist" is meaningless. Irresponsible opportunists who make it a practice to attack every person or group with whom they disagree as "Communists" have actually aided their supposed "enemies."

An example of what the committee is driving at shows very clearly in a recent story distributed by the United Press and which appeared in late editions of the *World-Telegram* last Monday, the day the hearing entered its second week. But this was an entirely different story: Senator [Ralph Owen] Brewster, as chairman of a Senate aviation subcommittee, had quite properly asked for an investigation into the airplane accident in Utah in which fifty-two persons were killed. So the United Press story began as follows: "Senator Brewster indicated today he believes sabotage by Communists may have been responsible for the accident." But whatever he may have had in mind, the Senator did not use the word "Communists." We checked up, and what he did say was, "In view of the ideological cold war now going on, the possibility of sabotage should not be overlooked." That was enough for the United Press, and that was twisted so that the hurried reader got the idea that Senator Brewster was blaming Communists for the airplane accident. Real, card-carrying comrades must have got quite a snicker out of that one.

Well, since the Thomas investigation involved Hollywood,

reporters couldn't be blamed for treating the affair cinema-style, with such comments as, "Showing tomorrow, Robert Taylor, standing room only." Or, "Performance today: Adolph Menjou." *CBS Views the Press* has caught a bit of the spirit, and we announce herewith on our marquee: "Next week, big scandal: the Lady in Mink."

## November 8, 1947

Don Hollenbeck's press criticism was unusual in the attention it paid to newspapers' use of words. The language of headlines and stories could be as important as the actual content of the articles. So Hollenbeck devoted parts of many broadcasts to skewering pretentious ten-dollar words (such as "aposiopesis" and "susurrus"), clichés, and unnecessary words.[1] Reporters preferred "a lone bandit" to "a bandit." Hollenbeck said, "It reminds us of a story we read once: A solitary horseman shows up on the horizon. Then another one shows up, and pretty soon the place is simply alive with solitary horsemen."[2] In this broadcast, Hollenbeck tackled a more significant use of language: the choice of words such as "divorcee" and "mink" in headlines to "distort the picture, to allow a mistaken impression to prevail."

AT THE CONCLUSION of last Saturday's broadcast, we announced that our topic for this week would be "The Lady in Mink"—a study of the latest developments in New York City's relief situation. The following Monday there arrived on our desk a copy of *Editor & Publisher*, the weekly magazine of the newspaper business. There was an editorial in that issue giving credit to the *World-Telegram* for beginning the crusade last spring which resulted in the current investigation, and the last two paragraphs of the editorial read as follows: "But a new type of radio program, *CBS Views the Press*, on May 31 called the original stories a 'great ink-letting' and a 'newspaper lynching party.' They called the incident 'about as sorry an exhibition as the press is capable of putting on.' It

1. On the use of "aposiopesis," see *CBS Views the Press*, September 27, 1947, transcript, 10; on the use of "susurrus," see *CBS Views the Press*, June 4, 1949, transcript, 3; on the use of clichés, see *CBS Views the Press*, July 23, 1949, transcript, 6–7.
2. *CBS Views the Press*, October 11, 1947, transcript, 11.

will be interesting to see if the producers of this radio program now have the courage to admit they jumped at conclusions five months ago and that the *World-Telegram*, object of their criticism then, has really performed a public service."

The producers of this radio program have the courage to admit that an investigation into the affairs of the Relief Administration seems called for on the basis of evidence uncovered by the *World-Telegram*. It was the manner in which the evidence was presented to the public which inspired the terms "ink-letting" and "lynching party." In the current case, the producers of *CBS Views the Press* have the courage to say that, in some aspects, this has been an even greater newspaper lynching party, and this time, the lynching party can chalk up to its credit a five-year-old girl.

Before we get to that, we're going to talk for a moment about WORDS. There are certain words and phrases which are described as "highly charged." They are words and phrases which set up in the mind of one who reads or hears them definite and violent reactions. They are words and phrases which represent things forbidden to most of us, and so the reactions they set up are those of envy and jealousy. Take the words "emerald" and "butler," for instance. Not many of us can afford to have square-cut emeralds or obsequious butlers, so when we read or hear about anybody who does have them, deep within us we may envy and dislike that person. A little reflection will bring to mind other highly charged words, but today—in connection with the relief story—we have to deal with one in particular. It is the word "mink." Not many of us can afford mink, either, and when the word is printed or spoken, our inner beings get a picture of forbidden luxury that is almost impossible to eradicate.

What a picture she is, the Lady in Mink. As slim-necked, haughty, and scented as a creature in *Vogue*; contemptuous of the lower classes; undoubtedly sporting a ten-carat emerald; and snooting her butler. Probably has a Rolls-Royce, too, or a Bentley. A lot of highly charged words are instantaneously called to mind just at the sight or sound of the word "mink."

Now the word "relief" is not a highly charged word. We don't envy people on relief; if we have any social conscience at all, we try to better their lot, and we accept the responsibility of providing care for them. There are a great number of people on relief in New York City, and that number is increasing. Two hundred sixty-three thousand is about the figure, and the department's caseload has increased 37 percent since V-J Day. As was pointed out in the original broadcast about the relief story, the great majority of these persons receive $1.31 a day, broken down as follows: 65¢ for food, 21¢ for clothes, 22¢ for rent, 23¢ for other needs. Like emeralds or mink coats. It might be pointed out that the buying power of this largesse has decreased, too; you don't get as many emeralds for a quarter as you used to.

On Wednesday, October 29, it developed at the state's hearing into the Relief Administration that a woman wearing a mink coat, who had received in 1940 a divorce settlement of $60,000, had been granted relief to the tune of $222 a month. On the face of it, a sad state of affairs. Mink versus relief: the two just simply don't go together, and as proof of the confusion that resulted, the afternoon editions of that day's newspapers didn't register their reactions to the highly charged word—comparatively dull was the *Sun*'s banner line saying, "Inquiry bares relief abuse."

The Lady in Mink didn't get mentioned until the subordinate part of the headline. No, it remained for the editors with more leisure to consider all implications and proportions of the story to react violently to the word "mink"—the editors of Thursday morning's papers. In the *Daily News,* in type an inch and a half high, this: "Divorcée in mink on relief rolls." Another highly charged word there—"divorcée." One almost adds the word "gay" to it—it connotes raciness in the extreme, with champagne out of slippers and forbidden naughtiness. But it remained for the *New York Times* of that same morning to illustrate what is meant by the reactions to a highly charged word, which, incidentally, is a very potent headline word, too. It usually takes a pretty important story to command in the *New York Times* on the right-hand side of page 1 a three-column headline in thirty-six-point Cheltenham bold condensed italic type with four cross-bars and banks.

Yet there it was: "Woman in mink with sixty thousand dollars lived on relief in a hotel, inquiry by state discloses." The commuter coming in from Teaneck or Westchester county or Long Island or Trenton, faced with the problem of paying an insurance premium or an installment on the mortgage, could scarcely be blamed for reacting violently—if divorcées in mink were going to live richly at the expense of the taxpayers, what was this country coming to? About the nearest his own wife would ever get to a mink coat would be to look longingly at those advertisements on pages 2 and 3 of the Sunday *Times*, and by gosh, it made a fellow sore the things people got away with.

The city Welfare Department also reacted violently to the word "mink" and got busy at once, with the result most of us know by now: the case was examined thoroughly, the coat in particular, and it turned out to be what finicky women describe as a rag they wouldn't be caught dead in. In all fairness, newspaper editors couldn't be blamed for playing up big at first a story about a woman with sixty thousand dollars and a mink coat drawing relief money—it was a shocking thought. But as it developed, the newspapers had been victimized; they had been furnished with incomplete data. That they could have had it all was proved by the case of one reporter: before Commissioner Fielding made his announcement that the Lady in Mink was entitled to relief, this reporter had called the Welfare Department and in three minutes had learned that there were extenuating circumstances. The Lady in Mink was found to be flat broke, clearly entitled to relief, and because of one of those silly laws, it was required that her five-year-old child be cared for; perhaps not even the angry commuter scanning the headlines would object to that. Even though the newspapers printed the findings of the investigation, they gave them by no means the prominence they gave the phony story, and the damage had been done, the implications remained, and for all that she was stony broke, living with her child in a rooming house, she continued in many headlines and stories to be the Lady in Mink.

This is by no means intended to be a defense of the Lady in Mink, her character, or her conduct. Perhaps she squandered her money; perhaps she didn't conform to the ideal of the sober, industrious citizen who wants to earn a living. The point is that by going gunning for mink, the newspapers had given the impression that to live on relief was to indulge in a sort of Lucullan life at the expense of the taxpayers. In the original stories, there were continued references to high life; an investigator had looked at the woman's coat with awe; the *Herald Tribune* described her as having a penchant for luxury; to the *Mirror* reporter she was haughty, living in a swank hotel; the *News* kept harping on the word "deluxe"; and so on. All incandescent, highly charged words, setting up automatic anger against conspicuous spending and conspicuous leisure.

They tended to make one ignore the larger picture: the fact that most of the 263,000 persons on relief today get about a $1.31 a day—that, as Albert Deutsch pointed out in *PM* the other day, while the chiselers and cheats make the headlines, very little, if anything, will be said about the tens of thousands of genuinely needy children, cripples, and infirm aged who are being cheated by inadequate relief budgets. These unfortunates, Mr. Deutsch said, don't make good copy, and they don't seem to fit into the "case" which the state investigating counsel is investigating. *PM*, incidentally, was about the only newspaper which seemed to be aware of its conscience in this affair; Mr. Deutsch and John Weiss of its staff at all times were at pains to point out that relief was not quite the continuing Petronius banquet we were being led to believe it was.

Almost lost sight of in the sensation-mongering was the real meaning of the statement by Mayor O'Dwyer's executive committee, which was sharply critical of the welfare administration. That report made the following points, duly reported in the press: (1) there was an overall lack of proper administrative control with regard to public assistance processed through local welfare centers; (2) the procedures and methods practiced in administering public assistance were found in many instances to be inefficient and wasteful.

Those are the covering points; the report implemented them with facts and figures, and on the basis of that report, a full and fair investigation into the Relief Administration was obviously called for. *The World-Telegram* had already pointed out many of the deficiencies and inefficiencies outlined in the report of the mayor's committee, and for this job, the *World-Telegram* is to be commended for performing a service in the interest of more efficient and less costly public relief. But where the *World-Telegram* and the rest of the newspapers trailing along at its heels cannot be commended is in their completely false implication that the deficiencies, inefficiencies, stupidities, and worse cover the 263,000 people on relief. A sincere job of public service in this respect would have investigated some dozens or hundreds of cases representative of those thousands on relief—would have attempted to portray a true state of affairs, where relief recipients of the largest city of the richest country in the world are living on standards below health and security.

Such an investigation would have pointed out how they live, the conditions of their housing, what happens to their children—even if their mothers happen to own ratty old mink coats. The *World-Telegram* itself is keenly aware of all this, as Walter MacDonald, who has been conducting the relief crusade, wrote. In the early days of the campaign, Mr. MacDonald said, referring to the *World-Telegram*, "This newspaper has never aimed to deprive deserving and needy persons of all the assistance they need. But we believe the public should know what's going on in the Welfare Department." An admirable charter, and under it, a newspaper might have done a job entitling it to a Pulitzer Prize, without victimizing some of our more unfortunate fellow citizens and without tending, by the use of sensational, highly charged words and phrases, to obscure the entire situation and to prejudice the minds and harden the hearts of people against all relief.

Perhaps the Hutchins committee on the freedom of the press supplies a guide to understanding with its comment, "The owners and managers of the press determine which persons, which facts, which versions of the facts, and which ideas shall reach the public."

One more quotation from this freedom of the press report:

> To attract the maximum audience, the press emphasizes the exceptional rather than the representative, the sensational rather than the significant. Many activities of the utmost social consequence lie below the surface of what are conventionally regarded as reportable incidents. . . . The effort to attract the maximum audience means that each news account must be written to catch headlines. The result is not a continued story of the life of a people but a series of vignettes, made to seem more significant than they really are. The sum of such discontinuous parts does not equal the whole because the parts have not been represented in their actual size and color in relation to the whole.

That is rather professorial language, but it is made plain as day by the case of the journalistic job done on the Lady in Mink: a lurid vignette has been furnished, to the extent that, by repeated references to her parenthood, a child has been lynched. One doesn't imagine that the five-year-old daughter of the Lady in Mink will be keeping a scrapbook of news stories about her in 1947.

## November 29, 1947

On rare occasions, Hollenbeck devoted *CBS Views the Press* to profiling an unusual journalist. Billy Rose—born in the Bronx on September 6, 1899, as William Samuel Rosenberg—first achieved fame at age sixteen as America's fastest stenographer. Later he became a well-known writer or cowriter of lyrics for four hundred songs, including "It's Only a Paper Moon," "More Than You Know," and "Me and My Shadow." As a theatrical impresario, he produced *Jumbo* (a 1935 circus musical starring Jimmy Durante, elephants, aerialists, and a Richard Rodgers and Lorenz Hart score) and *Carmen Jones* (a 1943 musical version of the opera *Carmen* with an all-black cast). The five-foot-three showman, who married and divorced five times, also operated a series of nightclubs, including Billy Rose's Diamond Horseshoe, which led to his "Pitching Horseshoes" syndicated column.[1] A dispute over how much of the column Rose actually wrote was all the news angle Hollenbeck needed to make Rose the subject of his broadcast.

THIS IS GOING TO BE a success story—the story of a man who has been described by Bernard M. Baruch, a former employer, as typical of America, with a thorough understanding of human nature, with independence, and courage. It is the success story of Billy Rose; not Billy Rose the saloon-keeper, not Billy Rose the songwriter, producer, or broadcaster, but Billy Rose the newspaper columnist. He's been pitching horseshoes with his column since April of last year, when there appeared in the *Daily News* an advertisement for the Diamond Horseshoe, a glit-

1. See "Billy Rose Is Dead; Showman Was 66," *New York Times*, February 11, 1966; and William Stephenson, "Rose, Billy," in *American National Biography*, vol. 18, ed. John A. Garraty and Mark C. Carnes, 858–60 (New York: Oxford University Press, 1999).

tering nightclub operated by Mr. Rose. He had complained to his advertising agency that he didn't seem to be getting his money's worth out of the two thousand dollars a week he was putting out to induce people to spend money in his place, so, in his own words, he decided to cook up some ads that would start selling some whisky. That first advertisement read, in part, as follows: "This is the first of a series of little pieces I intend to run in this gazette. I shall publicly deliver myself of miscellaneous notions on Life, Art, Reforestation, and Sex Among the Aborigines. The purpose of these pipsqueak paragraphs will be not so much to improve the mind of the populace as to inveigle it into my Diamond Horseshoe."

That was the beginning, but the commercial motive was quickly submerged under a flood of literary chit-chat about everything under the sun except Mr. Rose's interest in selling whisky. As of now, instead of paying to get his stuff into the papers, Mr. Rose is guaranteed by 181 newspapers a total of fifty-two thousand dollars a year for his little pieces and miscellaneous notions. On January 1, his column will move from the newspaper *PM*, where he really got his start, to the *Herald Tribune*. You might call it a rags-to-riches story, speaking strictly of Mr. Rose as a columnist. He had been, and is, doing very much all right in other fields of endeavor before he got into journalism.

Few columns have caught on as quickly as Mr. Rose's did, and *CBS Views the Press* views Mr. Rose as a phenomenon of the newspaper business. He has been called fabulous, incredible, a man with a Midas touch. Maybe he is all that in show business, but looked at from a journalistic standpoint, he's clever with words and ideas, a man who has heard and read much, whose mind has retained the best, and who is able to communicate it. One newsman has this to say of him: "Here is a guy with a tremendous amount of intellect and grasp, with ability to deal with all types and classes of people, with ability to speak my group's particular language, and to meet people on their own ground; a fascinating character who has what it takes, keeps the money angle right up close to the surface, but basically uses money as representative of what he really wants: pride and satisfaction, applause and respect." Indicative of that is Mr. Rose's extreme sensitivity to any suggestion that his literary output isn't strictly his own—that somebody else writes his stuff. That has come up occasionally, and it is one of the things about which Mr. Rose is touchiest. Here is his answer to it, in his own words:

> Broadway is the kind of street where if a guy earns more than two dollars, the pings are all out for him. Of course I'm not happy about the knocks—let 'em drop dead.
>
> I've been playing clay pigeon for a long time. Maybe they think I'm making too much dough, that I'm a loudmouth. After all, these guys are married; they bring home a fast hundred and a quarter, and a guy pops out from behind a rock and makes fifty-two Gs. So the wife says, "What goes with YOU, Jack?" So Jack goes out and writes about Rose: "What goes with YOU, Jack?" Maybe they're sore when I bought an art gallery. I got tired of railroad calendars on the wall, and I bought into Rembrandt.
>
> I bought the Ziegfeld Theater. They said, "Now he's gonna go on his nose." Take my house up there at Mount Kisco—thirty or forty rooms. They'd say, "Here's a kid out of the dust and mud of the East Side." They'd throw a stone rock through the windows. "A guy out of Delancey Street should be wearing knee britches and a powdered wig?" they'd say. Let 'em drop dead.

For a guy out of Delancey Street who has bought into Rembrandt and is figuratively wearing knee britches and a powdered wig, for a man who has many possessions, including assets estimated at five million dollars, it might seem difficult to pick out the possession of which he is proudest. Right now, Billy Rose gives the impression that it is the column of which he is proudest, and any hint that it is not all his own brings instant anger; his eyes smolder—let 'em drop dead. All his life, from childhood on, Billy Rose has fought and competed in a tough world where one makes a few friends but plenty of enemies. Mr. Rose is well aware that there are in his world plenty of people who hold him in low esteem and who try to sell him short whenever they can. But he is also well aware that his head is something more than a peg for his size-seven hat; it has brains in it, and the column represents those brains.

Since the time when, as Billy Rose says, he put his finger to the portable to write ads to sell more whisky, there is that success story of his column. He tells it this way: six weeks after the ads began running in the *Daily News*, he got a call from Ralph Ingersoll, then editor of *PM*.

Mr. Ingersoll offered to print them free, if he could have them a day before they ran in the *News*. Okay by Mr. Rose, and it gave him an idea. He called an editor friend of his in Fort Worth and offered him the same proposition. That clicked, too, and the columnar career had begun. As he says, "Now I was a big syndicate fellow. . . . I figured that if these would take it, there must be a lot of other hep guys." So Mr. Rose spent a dollar for a newspaper directory and began making long-distance telephone calls. Within a month he had forty-six papers, all printing the column free. Then one day in September, John Wheeler, head of the Bell Syndicate, called to see him. According to Mr. Rose, the dialogue went this way:

WHEELER: I'm gonna make a deal for the column this afternoon.

ROSE: Not hard to sell me. What you gonna give?

WHEELER: Fifty-two Gs guarantee.

ROSE: You're kidding.

WHEELER: No, I'm offering you that much to keep you in this column business seriously. I missed out on Will Rogers and O. O. McIntyre, and I don't want to miss out on this. I want to bottle it this afternoon.

They bottled it, and Mr. Wheeler got busy. By the end of the year, ninety newspapers were using the column free, and Mr. Wheeler signed up eighty-nine of them to pay cash money for it. Concerning that deal, Mr. Rose made the classic remark, "A pox on the one that got away." Not many more got away. Mr. Rose himself says he now appears in 193 papers, but the syndicate says it's 181—enough, anyway.

About the preparation of the column, Mr. Rose is at pains to point out that he has only about 10 percent of the research assistance other columnists have—bird-dog help, he calls it. He has two researchers and would like more—like *Time* magazine, he says, recalling the job that publication did on him last summer, his picture on the cover and everything. "It was like a swarm descending on me," he says. "Those eager beavers putting the eye on me—one looking through papers here, another investigating something there, a cameraman roving hither and yon. All of them insatiable, ever returning to their quarry. That's the kind of help I'd like to have—those bright young research assistants on *Time*." Others who have been interviewed by *Time* report much the same experience as Mr. Rose, but now to get back to his own job.

About the help he does have, Mr. Rose says this: "Got a lot of sweet people around. But the minute we get a thunderhead, I kiss him good-bye." Some of the sweet people who are working for Mr. Rose now are Milton Subotsky and Lynn Jones, both of them researchers (Mr. Subotsky on a part-time basis; he recently spent many hours in the public library looking up the habits of pigeons for a "Pitching Horseshoes" column). There's the secretary, Helen Schrank, who has been with Mr. Rose about five years, and the press agent, Charles Washburn, who has been there at various times since 1930 and who used to be a newspaperman himself. All these people call each other and everybody else "honey" and "sweetheart" in the tradition of Broadway. Until recently, Lee Rogow had been on the Rose staff; he had originally worked for the advertising agency which handled Mr. Rose's account. He resigned last month and has been negotiating with *PM* to do a column of his own for that paper when "Pitching Horseshoes" goes over to the *Herald Tribune.*

The present Rose staff works on the seventh and eighth floors of the Ziegfeld Theater building at Sixth Avenue and Fifty-fourth Street. Mr. Rose occupies the office of the late Florenz Ziegfeld, and office hours are irregular. Mr. Rose himself works from ten o'clock in the morning until midnight. He puts in an average of two to five hours a day on the column. He says he first writes it in shorthand, then dictates to a stenographer. After that, he puts what Ernest Hemingway calls the junk detector on it. Such as, "Dawn was graying the window shades. Just say it was morning." After the junk detector test, Mr. Rose manicures the piece—puts the finishing touches to it—and sends it to the syndicate.

Concerning the readability of what comes out of this process, we have an expert opinion: that of Vincent S. Jones, executive editor of the *Utica (New York) Observer-Dispatch* and the *Utica Daily Press.* Mr. Jones is recognized in his profession as being eminently qualified to discuss good newspaper writing. And of Billy Rose's column Mr. Jones says, "It's interesting to see how it breaks down into short sentences, few complex words, and a very high proportion of human-interest words. No yardstick can measure the man's shrewd choice of descriptive words or the deft twist he applies to everything. Utica is 225 miles from Broadway, but Rose's stuff seems to have the widest appeal of anything we ever ran. More power to him." That's the formula for making a guarantee of fifty-two thousand dollars a year out of a column.

"I'm doing what I always wanted to do," says Billy Rose, and he keeps coming back to those hints that he doesn't do all this himself. It worries him that people could think this of him, although he dismisses it à la Broadway when he says, "I'd like to hire somebody to do it. I've got the dough. . . . I want to see my wife—what good is all this dough? As she says, we don't get to spend it, we're not having fun." But, to quote him again, "This writing business is a big plateful of ego." And of the writers who offend that ego, he says, "Writers can write better pieces tearing a guy down than singing songs about him. Despite the fact that I've read more, been more places, traveled with better people, some of these articles make me out an ungrammatical yahoo."

Mr. Rose's plateful of ego has been heaped to overflowing in the past few days because the Russians are mad at him. He wrote a piece once in which he said he didn't believe we needed to worry about the Russians hitting us with an atomic bomb because he didn't think the Russians have what it takes to figure one out. In Rose prose, they didn't know the difference between borscht and lubricating oil. The *Moscow Literary Gazette* responded by calling the columnist, among other things, an illiterate yellow journalist, a rogue from Broadway. "Great," says Mr. Rose. "Better than a medal from the Columbia School of Journalism."

The reading and people in Billy Rose's life have included large chunks of O. Henry, DeMaupassant, and Molnar—for the latter he has intense admiration. The people to whom he says he has given twenty years of ear time are Ben Hecht, Gene Fowler, Charles MacArthur, Damon Runyon, Quentin Reynolds. These are the people and reading which have influenced Billy Rose, but he has added his own vivid English to the pitch of the horseshoe. Some ideas for each day's pitch come from his mailbag, many of them out of personal reminiscence, and the prototype of Major Timothy Morgan, with his grandiose jabberwocky, is an extraordinary real-life press agent.

Major Morgan and other Rose characters will appear only about a month more in *PM*; they move then to the *Herald Tribune*, and Mr. Rose is highly pleased. As he says, "It's a red feather in my writing cap—what writer wouldn't want to work for the *Herald Tribune*?"

Writers of articles about Billy Rose almost invariably speculate about the man's motivation—the reason for his being the phenomenon he is. It isn't easy to get the answer from Billy Rose himself; it's one of the few questions to which he doesn't have a ready reply. "I don't know," he says. "Everybody's got a pocketful of hot needles—you've got a pocketful of hot needles. I've just got into that daffy kind of rhythm. Writing this column has finally given me a chance in life to do what I really want to do." And then he adds what would undoubtedly be graven on his escutcheon if he had one, a motto which Billy Rose has learned the hard way in the forty-eight years from Delancey Street to Mount Kisco and a share in Rembrandt. "I play," Billy Rose says, "winner take all."

## December 13, 1947

Hollenbeck believed that a good newspaper encouraged a no-holds-barred discussion with its readers. Letters to the editor were opportunities for readers to criticize as well as compliment the coverage and commentary in newspapers. In this broadcast, Hollenbeck captured some of the ironies—some might say hypocrisies—involved in how newspaper editors treated letters from their readers. A *New York Daily News* editor, insistent that a magazine editor could not change a word of his letter to the editor, aggressively cut letters to his own paper to sentence-long snippets. William Randolph Hearst wrote eloquently about "free discussion to establish the truth" being "the very life sustaining blood stream of democracy." The press, said Hearst, "must open columns to free and illuminating discussion."[1] But when it came to the publication of letters to the editor, Hearst's *Journal-American* and *Mirror* exhibited a contrary approach.

WRITING LETTERS TO THE EDITOR is an old and honorable custom—as old as newspapers themselves and, in fact, almost the beginning of newspapers. In earlier times, when communications were more leisurely, letters to the editor often brought the news itself. Now and then they still do, but in modern times, the letters to the editor more often bring reactions to the news or to a newspaper's editorial position. For one reason or another, most newspapers publish as many of the letters they receive as they can, and a recent random poll by the trade magazine *Editor & Publisher* revealed that editors gave the following reasons for printing these communications: (1) because they uphold the

1. William Randolph Hearst, "Propaganda," June 13, 1941, quoted in *Selections from the Writings and Speeches of William Randolph Hearst* (San Francisco: private publisher, 1948), 351.

editorial opinion of the paper; (2) because they offer a valuable criticism; (3) because they solicit aid for a worthy cause; and (4) because they themselves are news. It is interesting to note that the first reason given is that the letters are printed because they uphold the newspaper's own editorial position; our discussion will throw some light on that matter. Letters to the editor are news these days. People seem to be writing more of them than they ever have before, and to quote Samuel Grafton in the *Post* the other day, "I have been in this business eighteen years, but never before have I received such hot and bitter letters as have come in during the last few days." Not all the letters to all the editors are hot and bitter, but in what the *Herald Tribune* has called these edgy times, people are very much aware of problems and are writing to the editors about them.

Reuben Maury, chief editorial writer of the *Daily News*, who supervises that newspaper's letters column, says that last year the paper got about 46,000 letters for publication but that the mail is running much heavier this year—about 150 letters a day, which would increase the annual receipt by 10,000. The *News*'s letter column, which it calls "Voice of the People," is one of the brightest and breeziest of any newspaper correspondence column and, as such, is widely read. Mr. Maury says it's among the top twenty *News* features which men like most to read and for women, among the top ten. Most of the *News* letters, Mr. Maury says, are from readers who disagree with an editorial or the handling of a news story. When the *News* first came out editorially against the five-cent fare, there were lots of squawks in the "Voice of the People." But now that Mayor O'Dwyer has called for an increase, Mr. Maury says that the mail shows the letter writers to be in favor of the increase, too; perhaps those against it have just given up and are thinking of other subjects about which to write to the editor. Most of the letters in the "Voice of the People" column are rewritten because of limitations of space. Mr. Maury used to do this himself, but the job is now handled by his assistant,

Donald Thompson. Letters-to-the-editor people are usually a wordy lot, and the *News* achieves that spirit of punch and brevity by doing them over, retaining the original meanings, suggestions, or criticisms. In the nearly twenty years the letters column has been appearing, Mr. Maury says they've had very few complaints about this rewriting treatment.

But about his own letters to the editor, Mr. Maury has other views. Last summer he had occasion to write to the editor of the *Nieman Reports*, a publication of the newspapermen and -women who are given fellowships at Harvard University. Mr. Maury was complaining about a reference to himself in the *Reports*, and at the end of his own letter to the editor, he appended the following curt notice: "Kindly publish the above piece of my literary property as is or not at all."

Mr. Maury's behest was obeyed. He was neither rewritten nor abridged as was, for example, a Brooklyn correspondent of the *News* signing himself John Abbenante. Following the Louis-Walcott fight, Mr. Abbenante wrote an indignant letter to the "Voice of the People," twenty-five lines of script in all. It was boiled down to the following: "Well, here's one guy who will never watch another professional fight as long as he lives." Sixteen words from probably a hundred and fifty. Mr. Maury and Mr. Thompson say that editorial policy does not govern the selection of material for the "Voice of the People." Those selections, they say, are made simply on the basis of what they think will interest the readers: humor, good ideas, sometimes slaps at the people and things the *News* is against. Kicks are always welcome; it's an ancient journalistic theory that there's more news value in an attack than there is in a defense of the status quo, and examination of the *News*'s letter column will show that it is predominately kicks about something or other. The *News*'s efforts to keep its letters column snappy and up among the top features leads it to some surprising stuff; things appear in the letters column which would never see print otherwise, the laws of libel and good taste being what they are. A woman reviles her neighbor in terms little short of slanderous; references are made to anatomy which would have a difficult time on the copy desk; insult is common, and people are "rats," "skunks," "weasels," and "bums." This type of letter naturally is signed with a false name, a practice which some newspapers do not permit. That's the *Daily News*'s way of running a letters column, but there are others.

The Hearst way, for instance. In the *Journal-American* there is a small space—the smallest on the editorial page—devoted to the editor's mailbox. In this space there appears usually one letter, not more than three. Almost without exception, these letters support the *Journal*'s editorial policies—anti-Communism, pro–military training, antivivisection, and so on. But there are other letter columns in the Hearst newspapers given much more prominence. These are from organizations and individuals who are profoundly grateful to William Randolph Hearst and his newspapers for something or other they have done. The *Mirror* almost never prints letters to the editor, but it printed one the other day from Adm. Chester W. Nimitz—a testimonial thanking the Hearst organization for its part in making Navy Day a success last October. The admiral singled out for admiration the work of Harry Schlacht and Nick Kenny, who between them contribute to the Hearst newspapers some of the most emotional printed matter to be found these days. Mr. Kenny's doggerel lyrics are sometimes in an old ballad form known as "sixes and eights" and are simple compared to Mr. Schlacht's output, which almost defies description but which Mr. Schlacht himself calls poetic prose; it is a mixture of prose, poetry, and blank verse and is extremely inspirational. Being inspirational is Mr. Schlacht's main job for the Hearst newspapers, for which he has been an editorial writer for ten years. He managed to work Admiral Nimitz's name into his Navy Day effusion, which may account for the admiral's bread-and-butter letter to the editor.

The testimonial character of the Hearst letters column is often carried to an extreme length. In an issue last month, one-third of the editorial page was devoted to communications from those praising Mr. Hearst for the promotion of a history competition among high school students. One of the favorite correspondents of Mr. Hearst is William Griffin, editor and publisher of a journalistic curiosity called the *New York Enquirer*, which appears on the newsstands Sunday afternoons. Mr. Griffin and Mr. Hearst think alike on a number of matters, and every now and then Mr. Griffin writes a letter to Mr. Hearst out in California, which Mr. Hearst then orders his newspapers to print.

The Hearst newspapers represent the extreme example of using letters from readers to support the paper's editorial policy. Over a recent six-week period, the *Journal-American* printed about fifty letters to the editor, not one of them opposed to Hearst policy. There may be other kinds of letters to Hearst editors, but they seldom see the light of day.

The most spirited and literate development in the field of letters to the editor has been inspired by an editorial in the *Herald Tribune* on Thanksgiving Day suggesting that employees should be required to state their beliefs in order to hold their jobs. That editorial brought some distinguished names in the list of letter writers to the editor. E. B. White of the *New Yorker* was first to respond with a dissent, and other opinions followed, pro and con. James Thurber got into it, Roger Angell, William Rose Benet, Robert W. Coates, and others. And on the principle that these letters made news, the *Herald Tribune* got the story into the front-page class by getting the opinions of Morris Ernst and Arthur Garfield Hayes, who were on opposite sides of the question. The *Herald Tribune* printed more letters in support of Mr. White's opinion than it did in favor of its own, sticking pretty closely to the proportion of the letters received. Geoffrey Parsons, who, as chief editorial writer, is boss of the *Herald Tribune* letters column, says the first mails brought about four letters against the *Herald Tribune*'s editorial to one in favor of it but that a recapitulation yesterday showed that the letters against the editorial had been reduced to a ratio of about two-to-one. He added that one of the principal reasons for using the letters column is to print criticism—a somewhat different point of view from that prevailing on the Hearst newspapers.

The White versus *Herald Tribune* controversy concerned ideas, their spread, and their control, and that discussion has taken on lately a comic touch—quite literally. In an effort to pep up its heavily class-conscious pages—and to get more readers—the *Daily Worker* in October began printing comic strips: *Reg'lar Fellers* by Gene Byrnes, *The Nebbs* by Stanley and Betsy Baer, *Virgil* by Mrs. Len Klies, and a reprinted series of cartoon commentaries by Gluyas Williams. A cry of pain at once went up from the Baers and from Mr. Byrnes; they weren't going to have their comic characters appearing in any Communist newspaper. The *Worker* agreed to drop *The Nebbs* but said it would stand on its right to print *Reg'lar Fellers.* To that, Mr. Byrnes retorted he would begin putting anti-Communist propaganda into the comic unless the *Worker* gives it up. John Wheeler, head of the Bell Syndicate, which distributes Mr. Byrne's comic, thinks that might not be a bad idea; personally, he says, he'd like to see the artist put Foreign Minister Molotov in the strip and make a heel out of him. Because, Mr. Wheeler says, that's what he is. And so it goes: from Hollywood to the funny papers.

Conditions in Palestine are serious, and they have been getting worse; all the news accounts from there make that pretty plain, and it would seem there is small reason to try to whoop the story up beyond its real proportions. Last Tuesday, under the signature of Robert Miller, the United Press sent into newspaper and radio offices a dispatch under a Jerusalem dateline which began as follows: "British authorities reported today that the Jewish Haganah defense army killed seventy Arabs and wounded one hundred others in a counterattack last night in the blood-soaked battleground between Tel Aviv and Jaffa." No other news agency or radio reporter confirmed that story, so we asked our Palestine correspondent Farnsworth Fowle how come. I'm going to quote Farnsworth's cabled reply, which we've just received: "Monday night, as a climax to the border troubles between Arab Jaffa and Jewish Tel Aviv, the Arabs staged a sort of banzai charge against a Haganah strongpoint. They were repulsed in darkness, but by next morning, the affray had mushroomed into one of the bloodiest encounters since Falstaff routed umpteen men in buckram. The only news agency staff correspondent in Tel Aviv was the United Press's Eliav Simon. Next morning, he found a British constable at the scene estimating that seventy Arabs had been killed, and Haganah had an even higher figure."

Prudence might have suggested these sources could be wrong, but anyway, Mr. Simon filed a dispatch crediting the figure of seventy to "British authorities"—meaning that constable. There is no censorship of outgoing press dispatches, so it reached New York and the world in time to create a considerable flap by the time it got back to Palestine. The British government in London was irritated at what it called "wild stuff" ascribed to British authorities, and the British secretariat in Palestine thereupon began yelling for the scalp of Robert Miller of the United Press. Why Mr. Miller? Because, Farnsworth says, it is the informal practice of news agencies on any running story coming from two staff members to use only one signature on day stories, another on night stories, regardless of which of them actually signs the cables. Now the British are after Mr. Simon. He has been notified that his credentials will be withdrawn unless he provides a satisfactory explanation. There has been other bitterness over coverage of the trouble in Palestine. The *Palestine Post*, one of the country's largest English-language dailies, referred editorially the other day to news correspondents on the scene as "foreign ghouls" and jibing at a dispatch by Carter Davidson of the Associated Press, in which Mr. Davidson gave an account of a wild ride he had during which his car was struck by a bullet. And the road, Mr. Davidson's dispatch said, was virtually knee-deep in stones flung at automobiles.

Now, Farnsworth says, the correspondents have formed a foreign-ghouls' association in their pressroom in Jerusalem, and the latest writer elected to membership has been the *Palestine Post*'s own correspondent in Haifa, who on Wednesday described that city as a battlefield, which it was not. Again, the situation in Palestine is serious. Farnsworth Fowle's account of what happened with just one story simply demonstrates how reporters can make even bad matters seem worse by their anxiety to get a whopping big story.

## May 22, 1948

Today, from Mexico to the Middle East, American correspondents are targets of kidnappers and assassins. So this broadcast about the murder in Greece of George Polk, CBS's Middle East correspondent, resonates with relevance. Just as Greek officials had been trying to get Polk transferred or fired before his murder, so, too, have U.S. correspondents seeking the truth in Iraq, Russia, and other world trouble spots been threatened or killed. In addition to *CBS Views the Press,* Hollenbeck and Edward R. Murrow (the only CBS newscasters who had consistently communicated with Polk by cable, letter, and telephone) enlisted the help of other CBS correspondents to produce four half-hour broadcasts in 1948–49 that investigated who was responsible for Polk's murder. The final program in April 1949 included Hollenbeck's report on investigations of the murder of Polk, as well as Winston Burdett's report on the Athens trial of Polk's accused killers—two Greek Communists in absentia and Gregory Staktopoulos, who was sentenced to life.[1] Murrow ended the program by describing Polk in words that also described Hollenbeck: "One of those reporters who believed that the pursuit of truth will set you free even if you never catch up with it."[2]

ONE OF THE LAST JOBS CBS correspondent George Polk did in Greece before he was murdered was another phase of an assignment to which he had devoted the nearly fifteen years of his career as a newsman: the search for truth. The truth about George

1. Despite the conviction of Staktopoulos, the identity of Polk's murderer remains a topic of debate. See Kati Marton, *The Polk Conspiracy: Murder and Cover-up in the Case of CBS News Correspondent George Polk* (New York: Farrar, Straus and Giroux, 1990); and Elias Vlanton, *Who Killed George Polk? The Press Covers Up a Death in the Family,* with Zak Mettger (Philadelphia: Temple University Press, 1996).
2. *CBS Reports: The Murder of George Polk,* April 27, 1949. Broadcast tape in the collection of MacDonald and Associates, Chicago.

Polk's death is not yet established; the evidence is incomplete, and we will have more to say on that point in a few minutes. What George Polk was trying to do before he went to Salonika to die with a bullet in the back of his head concerned criticism of another reporter in Greece, a reporter who, along with George Polk (and a lot of other reporters), has always tried to report not only the fact but the truth about the fact. That reporter is Homer Bigart of the *New York Herald Tribune*, whose correspondence to his newspaper has displeased the Greek government.

Now the correspondence of many reporters from Greece has displeased the Greek government—George Polk himself had reason to know this—but the Greek government's displeasure with Homer Bigart of the *Herald Tribune* had an unusual sequel: Dwight Griswold, the head of the American Mission for Aid to Greece, wrote a long letter of complaint to the editor of the *Herald Tribune* about Mr. Bigart's reporting, which he said was not factual.

Now this is bad business for a reporter, this writing letters to his boss about something he has done or is accused of having done. It tends to discredit the reporter, and even if the letter writer is wrong, it starts a fuss; the complaint has to be answered. If the criticism of the reporter is justified, of course the public airing of it is healthy. The reporter must say, "I take it back"; he must face up to his responsibility to tell the truth. But if the criticism is not justified, the original impression is never quite eradicated. It's the old story of the denial never quite catching up with the original statement, and the reporter, although he has satisfactorily answered his accuser, still wears a scar. In this case, there can be no attempt to judge the merits of the criticism. Mr. Bigart's answer is not yet on the record; he hasn't yet said, "I take it back" or, "I won't take it back."

Mr. Griswold's complaint about Mr. Bigart's reporting appeared in the *Herald Tribune* on May 2. It seemed pretty serious: Mr. Griswold took issue with Mr. Bigart's findings about Greece on a number of points, and the conclusion of his letter was particularly serious, since Mr. Griswold said the case reminded him of the recent visit to America of Ilya Ehrenburg, the Russian propagandist who had presented a distorted picture of our country. Mr. Griswold's point was that the Russian had reported—factually enough—only on the less attractive features of American life, and this was what Mr. Bigart seemed to be doing in Greece, yet the overall effect was to make a damaging allusion. Homer Bigart and Ilya Ehrenburg coupled in a reference which would seem to imply that they were birds of a feather, and the implication for the casual or thoughtless reader is that it's a red feather.

Mr. Bigart is preparing his own answer to Mr. Griswold's letter, but he is not preparing it in Greece. Mr. Bigart has been transferred temporarily to Belgrade—at his own suggestion, the *Herald Tribune* says, with the intention of going back to Greece later and resuming his job there. A month ago, the *Herald Tribune* says, Mr. Bigart expressed the opinion that there might be a better story to be gotten in Yugoslavia than there was in Greece at the moment. Mr. Bigart's judgment of news sources and possibilities is respected by his editors; he has been with the *Herald Tribune* since 1929, and in 1946 he won a Pulitzer Prize for his wartime reporting from the Pacific. In absenting himself from Greece at this particular time, Mr. Bigart has lost touch with one of the most important stories to come out of that country recently: Who killed George Polk, and why? Knowing Homer Bigart's devotion to the truth, one misses his reports on a story where the truth is so difficult to isolate. But to return to Mr. Bigart's own case.

Pending Mr. Bigart's answer to Mr. Griswold's letter, we asked George Polk for a comment, and a few days before he left Athens for Salonika, we had a cable from him and later a telephone conversation with him. In his cabled reply, Mr. Polk said that the Griswold-Bigart controversy was such as almost to preclude his taking sides. Both were his friends, Mr. Polk said; both are honest and sincere. But he went right to the heart of the matter when he made this observation: that the trouble seems to be a clash between the diplomatic versus the reporting aspects of the Greek situation, plus the entanglement of the official versus the unofficial attitudes.

And Mr. Polk's cable went on to point out that because of his important position, Mr. Griswold couldn't know about all the goings-on, whereas Mr. Bigart's nondiplomatic status enabled him to see the situation from the bottom up. And now to quote directly from George Polk's last cable to us: "Lacking guts to attack us openly, the Greek officials are working behind the scenes to get certain American reporters transferred or fired. For instance, while I've never been reproached by the numerous Greek press ministry officials whom I see constantly, yet the Greek press ministry has been actively seeking to discredit me for some time."

CBS had heard that there had been high-level attempts to get Homer Bigart transferred, and to this question, Mr. Polk said he could confirm that a number of persons—Greeks and non-Greeks—had tried to do so, that the Greek ambassador to Washington had pulled wires vigorously, that an American embassy official in Athens had protested Mr. Bigart's stories to a visiting *Herald Tribune* business executive. When the executive asked, "Is Mr. Bigart factually incorrect?" the reply was, "No, but the tone of the writing is unfriendly." Simultaneously, Mr. Polk's cable continued, top-level Greek government officials had sought to influence American-mission press attaché to arrange for Mr. Bigart's recall, and he went on to say that in his opinion, Homer Bigart might occasionally have over-written or sensationalized a situation that needs thorough ventilation. "Essentially," Mr. Polk said, "Bigart has only been trying to tear down the gobbledygook about the facade called Greek democracy."

One thing is clear from the Griswold-Bigart exchange, Mr. Polk went on, and that is where there's so much smoke, fanned by so many reporters, there's hot fire. The meaning of that is plain. Too many reporters have had run-ins with the Greek government for there not to be any fire. Seymour Freidden of the *Herald Tribune*, Robert Vermillion of the United Press, Constantine Poulos of the Overseas News Agency, Dana Adams Schmidt of the *New York Times*, Ray Daniell of the *New York Times*, Constantine Argyris of the *Christian Science Monitor*, John O'Donovan of the *London Observer*, Stephen Barber of the *London News Chronicle*, his wife Mary Barber of *Time* magazine, Fred Sparks of the *Chicago Daily News*—quite a roll call of correspondents who have felt the displeasure of the Greek government.

They have felt it in various ways: assignments have been made difficult, slander has been spread about them, open or covert efforts have been made to get them removed from the scene. Homer Bigart's apartment was ransacked, his assistant arrested. Or there will appear in an Athens newspaper a comment such as the following, for the translation of which I am indebted to Constantine Poulos: "How long," the newspaper asks, "must Greece continue to suffer the lies of these American correspondents who get their money from Moscow and their information from Red wenches?" These correspondents of course, including those named above, some of the best in the business, and others. The Red wenches would seem to be in pretty select company.

Now as for the Griswold letter: Mr. Polk's cable added that it was being released for publication in Athens and that he would advise us later as to its reception in Greece. He did so by telephone two days later. He told this reporter that, naturally enough, the Greek extreme right-wing elements had received the letter with whoops of joy and were busy turning it into a testimonial for themselves—also that its publication was going to make honest reporting just that much more difficult in Greece. He added that he was going up north and that he'd have more when he got back to Athens.

George Polk did not get back to Athens, and the reasons for his not getting back are, as said before, not yet entirely clear. Who murdered George Polk and why are two unanswered questions to which truthful answers must be found. First, of course, as a matter of justice, and second, because all reporters everywhere are vitally concerned—the bell tolls for them. Both extreme left and extreme right are using George Polk's death for propaganda purposes, and Radio Athens, the voice of Greek government of which George Polk was often critical, has gone on the air with the assertion that George Polk had always worked for the recognition of Greece's rights, that he held anti-Communist views, and therefore he must have been murdered by the Communists. For their part, the Communists say that Mr. Polk was murdered by the Greek government as a warning to reporters not to try to get in touch with the free Greek forces.

It is quite true that George Polk had been critical of the Greek government; it is just as true that he had been critical of the other side. As Edward R. Murrow put it the other night, "He spared neither the corruption, inefficiency, and petty political maneuvering of the Greek government, nor the vacillation of American policy, nor . . . the atrocities committed by the Communists. What happened he reported, without fear and in language that all could understand." To accuse George Polk of bias on one side or the other of the Greek question is to ignore the record of the work he left behind him. For either side to use him as a martyr or as an apologist is ghastly.

The Columbia Broadcasting System does not intend to be swayed by the propaganda of the Greek right, center, or left. It will be convinced only by hard facts—facts developed through an honest and intensive investigation into who is responsible for the death of George Polk.

George Polk told us long ago that there was a systematic campaign on the part of the Greek government against correspondents who try to report the facts as they found them; in the Bigart case, the new factor is the entry of American officialdom into the matter. We've reported a number of times on this program the difficulties of American newsmen, and the situation will bear some recapitulation. The campaign against the reporters is part of a larger one and is complicated by the fact that the Communists are attacking American policy in Greece, too; both right and left are charging us with the interference in internal Greek affairs. Both left and right want control; they don't like American reporters who send stories which threaten to upset their plans for assuming complete control of the country when the proper moment arrives.

To quote again from George Polk's last cable to us:

> Although there is ostensibly no censorship or press restriction in Greece, it's my opinion that this is not because the Greek government stoutly believes in providing such working conditions for reporters. Rather, it is because the Greek government does not want trouble with an American whose country supplies the money that keeps Greece going. As an example of how the Greek government really feels about freedom of the press, there is the case of a Dutch correspondent whose legation in Athens recently applied for a visa for him. The Greek press ministry granted the visa but bluntly informed the Dutch legation that one "unfriendly" story from the Dutch reporter would mean the loss of his visitor's permit.

The Netherlands, of course, are not supplying cash to Greece, and one may speak in firm tones to Dutch reporters.

Constantine Poulos, in an article written for the Overseas News Agency, puts it this way: The Polk case

> draws into sharper focus the difficulties and dangers facing American correspondents overseas, as well as the responsibilities of governments toward foreign reporters. As the United States rose to a preeminent position in world affairs after the war, so did the value of American public opinion and, naturally, the importance of American correspondents abroad.
>
> Thus, the men and women who reported to the American

> people on events and developments overseas came to be considered by the various European governments as Very Important Persons. Accordingly, these correspondents were either pampered or threatened, depending on whether they reported favorably or unfavorably about any particular government.

Mr. Poulos's observations would seem to point up the conscientious correspondent's problem of accurate reporting and interpretation in a country where he is expected either to be a press agent and apologist for the existing authority or, as he is expected to be in Soviet-dominated areas, an outright enemy and more than probably a capitalist spy. Objectivity in reporting is increasingly difficult; the record is full of cases where reporters attempting to tell the truth have been threatened, mistreated, slandered, and thrown out or lavishly adulated as salesmen for a particular ideology.

George Polk did not die to become a martyr or a rallying cry for any politician of whatever complexion; George Polk died because he was trying to find out the truth. In this case, he had indicated he wanted to get an interview with the leader of the Greek guerrilla forces; as he had told a friend, we've had lots of secondhand reports about what those people are doing, and he'd like to get the facts for himself. If the facts had been critical of the Communists, George Polk would have so reported them. If the facts had been critical of the Greek government, George Polk would have so reported them. He was an apologist for nobody.

But to repeat: all reporters everywhere are vitally concerned in finding the answer to the death of George Polk; the survival of truth and the free flow of news are at stake. In these days, when more and more obstacles are put in the paths of reporters who are trying to learn the truth and to communicate that truth to readers and to listeners, the murder of a good reporter is more than the death of one man; it is the murder of truth, and truth is having enough trouble surviving these days.

## June 19, 1948

Hollenbeck used this broadcast not only to explore reporters' racial sensitivity but also to examine reporters' relationships with their sources. Reporting textbooks ask the journalism student to question the reliability of a source: "Am I being manipulated for some reason?"[1] But the journalist, too, is capable of manipulating a source. Janet Malcolm began *The Journalist and the Murderer* with hyperbole: "Every journalist who is not stupid or too full of himself to notice what is going on knows that what he does is morally indefensible. He is a kind of confidence man, preying on people's vanity, ignorance, or loneliness, gaining their trust and betraying them without remorse."[2] Hollenbeck detailed how some reporters translate the innocent words of coroners, police officers, and other sources into sensational headlines that stereotype and mislead.

WHEN IS AN APE-MAN not an ape-man? One answer, perhaps, is: when he appears in New York newspaper headlines. The dictionary tells us that the ape-man's name is *Pithecanthropus erectus*—or Java man or ape-man—and is thought to be among the earliest arrivals of mankind on the face of the earth. And while the various encyclopedias are shy about saying just exactly what day in history the ape-man first made his appearance on the scene, they do place him in the Pleistocene age. And that means anything up to four hundred thousand years ago—give or take a couple of centuries. Decidedly ancient history. In fact, even more prehistory ancient than ancient. But our scientists—our geologists and anthropologists who spent years placing the ape-man in

1. Tim Harrower, *Inside Reporting: A Practical Guide to the Craft of Journalism* (New York: McGraw Hill, 2007), 69.
2. Janet Malcolm, *The Journalist and the Murderer* (New York: Alfred A. Knopf, 1990), 3.

the Pleistocene age of world history—are always open to new discoveries. And discovery it must have been when our newspapers recently came up with a new "ape-man"—not thousands of years old but of now, of this moment, of 1948. Frankly, we don't think the scientists went for this one.

Early this month, the police reported that a vicious crime had been committed in the Washington Heights neighborhood. A middle-aged woman had been assaulted and robbed, and the blows to her head soon resulted in her death. The robbery part of the crime was similar to many like it in the Washington Heights neighborhood, and the police placed added men on duty there in a concerted drive to find the criminal or criminals.

It was this setting that gave rise to the discovery of the new "ape-man." Because, shortly after reporters talked with police, the *Post*, *Journal*, and *Telegram* carried front-page headlines to the effect that police were hunting an "ape-man" as the murderer. And by the time the allegedly confessed murderer was taken into custody—one week later—the only papers that had *not* referred to him as "the ape-man" in headlines were the *Herald Tribune*, the *Sun*, and *PM*. At that, once the man was arrested, the papers had a hard time trying to make the "ape-man" description stick. The arrested man turned out to be a slim, medium-height young man. His demeanor, the *New York Times* said, was so timid that the police found it hard to believe his story. Appearances can be deceptive, however, and the arrested man was charged with numerous crimes, including murder.

But the "ape-man" story has created a disturbed feeling both among readers and working newspapermen. And the center of this disturbance is the fact that the arrested man happens to be a Negro. We say "happens" deliberately, because white men and yellow men and brown and red men are also arrested for vicious crimes. But the fact that the man is a Negro casts a new light on the "ape-man" description. People wonder out loud and in print whether the description was just the usual run-of-the-mill sensational headline words in a murder story or whether this was another example of Jim Crow journalism.

Negro newspapers in Harlem hit out hard at the "ape-man" story. The *New York Amsterdam News* poured its editorial emotions into its front-page news story on the arrest of the suspect and declared, "By calling the slayer an 'ape-man' in one sentence and later on in the stories calling him a Negro, the press and police succeeded in whipping up bitter racial feeling in the community and laid the basis for probable serious trouble in an area where good community and race relations presently exist." And Ludlow Werner, editor of the *New York Age*, wrote, "This . . . is a protest against the common practice among daily newspapers of characterizing as 'ape-like' every Negro suspected of attacking a white woman."

"Some Negro criminals are 'ape-like,'" Mr. Werner writes, "but so are some white criminals. And yet a white criminal is never called 'ape-like.' Oh no, that term is reserved exclusively for describing Negroes."

Mr. Werner's suggestion that any criminals—Negro or white—may be "ape-like" probably won't find favorable acceptance with most anthropologists who, after all, spend years of scientific research in clearing up just such myths of race and color. Nor is the press guilty of so wide an accusation as he makes. Nor does the Negro press itself refrain from some of the reprehensible techniques of the general-circulation newspapers. But all this simply adds up to what every schoolchild knows: that two wrongs do not make a right. And yet, the heart of Mr. Werner's criticism of the press in its treatment of Negroes springs from the real-life bitter experiences of a people that has long suffered the blows of so un-American and undemocratic a procedure as color discrimination.

Jim Crow journalism is still with us—although in greatly diminished strength compared to past years, when crimes involving Negroes assumed headline importance not so much because of the crime itself but because a Negro was involved. Time was in the movies, too, when a slanderous kind of so-called fun was poked at people because of their color or foreign accents, or the villain was a villain principally because he was crippled or disfigured. These are the harmful stereotypes that the press, movies, and radio have been making a determined effort to get away from—so much so, as James Thurber points out in his excellent *New Yorker* series on radio soap operas, that the hero there is a hero mainly because he goes through so many physical afflictions as to make the tribulations of Job pale by comparison.

We don't like to use Hollywood films to point up how newspaper work really goes on because the movies romanticize and exaggerate in that field too often. But every once in a while, a movie comes along that does contain a realistic scene portraying newspapermen at work. Perhaps you've seen *A Double Life*, where Ronald Colman portrays an actor who becomes so overwhelmed emotionally by his role of Othello that he strangles a lady friend while reciting that famous scene with Desdemona—the scene of a combination strangle and kiss. Later, a reporter speaks to the coroner and ferrets out this kissing possibility. The coroner is a meek man and isn't sure that the victim was kissed when strangled and doesn't want to be quoted as saying so.

But the reporter persists, promises big headlines quoting the coroner, and after a priceless scene of interview haggling, the coroner assents—and soon the papers are rolling off the press, blazoned with giant headlines reading, "Kiss of death, says coroner." This search for a sock phrase or description is not a rare habit with crime reporters, and from the evidence at hand, it seems that that's largely the way "Police hunt ape-man" headlines came about. According to the *Amsterdam News*, police headquarters denied releasing any "ape-man" description, but a police denial does not necessarily mean that the newspapers which quoted the police to that effect are wrong. The police are rarely in the habit of issuing written statements to reporters, and if a quotation subsequently becomes embarrassing, the police—like many officials in public life—can issue a denial, leaving the reporters and their papers holding the bag. There's a tacit understanding among all hands that these things are likely to happen, and it's a chance reporters have to take. From what we have learned, police personnel on the case told reporters the suspect was a hulking man over six feet tall, with huge shoulders and unnaturally long, dangling arms. At which, one reporter remarked, "Wait a minute; that description adds up to an ape-like character—an ape-man, wouldn't you say?" To which a police official replied, "Yes, ape-like." Bang! Big headlines in that afternoon's *Post*, *Telegram*, and *Journal* on the "ape-man."

The *Sun* ignored the description, but the *Post* was the only paper that afternoon not to identify the wanted man as a Negro. Some reporters and editors contend that when they get a police description that's good enough for a headline, they'll print it, regardless of the man's color. Other reporters and editors apparently have different ideas. In the first morning-paper stories the next day, four out of five papers—the *Herald Tribune*, *PM*, the *Times*, and the *News*—did not touch the ape-man description, and *PM* and the *Herald Tribune* did not consider the suspect's color to be a legitimate element of their stories. Wonder of wonders, the *Herald Tribune* simply stated that the police were looking for a murderer; no highly charged descriptive words were used, and still, the *Tribune*'s remarkably detailed story made the sensationalized-headline stories of the previous day's papers look rather amateurish indeed. As it turned out, when the suspect was arrested, the police were quoted to the effect that they had given out a misleading description as part of their strategy. But the "ape-man" description had been given quite a heavy circulation and had left a rather bad taste in the mouth around town. Tied in with the color designation, even with the purest of motives, it nevertheless set up a vicious stereotype which, as the *Amsterdam News* noted, may have "whipped up bitter racial feeling."

June 19, 1948

Our newspapers, backed by constitutional guarantees of freedom of the press, are often regarded as the major fortress of democracy. But no thoughtful observer has yet suggested that freedom of the press or democracy are enhanced by Jim Crow journalism, with one set of ethics for some Americans and another set for other Americans. Let's file all ape-man stories where they belong—in the folder that reads "*Pithecanthropus erectus,* Java man, Pleistocene epoch, four hundred thousand years ago . . . a couple of centuries more, a couple of centuries less."

## August 7, 1948

In 1954 Kenneth Tynan described Rebecca West, then at the peak of her luminous lucidity, as "the best journalist alive."[1] West began her writing career in England on the political left as a journalist, novelist, and literary critic, contributing in 1911 to the feminist *Freewoman* and then the socialist *Clarion*. But by the early 1950s, despite what she called "the demagogic qualities of Senator McCarthy," she was vigorously defending McCarthyism and the anti-Communism crusade in the United States.[2] In 1948, when she covered the three U.S. political conventions for the *New York Herald Tribune* and other newspapers, her more conservative politics began to show. Hollenbeck used this broadcast to criticize what he saw as bias in her coverage of the conventions. But the uncharacteristic ferocity of his criticism—his description of "the world's number-one woman-writer" as "middle fifties, graying, and stout" and his repeated references to her beautiful, purebred Jersey cows—raises the question of his own bias. Was he a bit of a misogynist as well as a misogamist? In twice quoting *Time* magazine about her looking "as if somebody had thrown her clothes on her," was he resorting to the same focus on appearance—on the superficial—that he was accusing her of using in her coverage of the convention delegates?

IT HAS BEEN FASHIONABLE in recent years among intellectuals and some working journalists to regard the British novelist Rebecca West as one of the top-flight reporters of our time. This department itself almost got lyrical about Miss West's reporting of the lynch trial at Greenville, South Carolina, for the *New Yorker*

1. Kenneth Tynan, as quoted in theater program for *That Woman: Rebecca West Remembers*, Manhattan Theatre Source, March 3–13, 2004, 6.
2. Rebecca West, "As a Briton Looks at 'McCarthyism,'" *U.S. News & World Report*, May 22, 1953, 79.

more than a year ago, but cooler counsel prevailed, and we finally decided that the palm for the reporting of that event should go to Robert S. Bird of the *Herald Tribune*. *Time* magazine some time ago characterized Miss West thus: "Most reporters report in one dimension, achieving at best the dramatic surface of a mural or a movie. Rebecca West reports in depth—a depth whose winding recesses of character, situation, and context she divines by the play of unusually acute instincts and intuitions guided by an eye for significant detail. And she floods the planes of her perception with the generous human warmth of a womanly nature and a culture-crowded brain that gives to the meanest fact a new perspective." The editors of the *Daily News* would call that a lot of seven-dollar prose and wouldn't be caught dead with it in their paper, but it is worth keeping in mind in an examination of Miss West's most recent reporting on the American scene: her job for the *Herald Tribune* and other newspapers at the three national conventions in Philadelphia. At Greenville, Miss West did seem to have those unusually acute instincts and intuitions so highly regarded by the *Time* critic; she did have the faculty of reporting in depth, and her perception caught details that other reporters missed or ignored.

Her reports of the three conventions got much greater circulation than did her stories from Greenville; the prestige of her name and of the newspapers in which the stories appeared assured them of wide and often uncritical reception. If Rebecca West saw it that way, it was so; to quote *Time* magazine again, she is indisputably the world's number-one woman writer. It may be brash to examine with a critical eye the output of the world's number-one woman writer, but some of her production at the conventions seems to call for it. First though, a brief biographical note about Rebecca West. She is in the middle fifties, graying, and stout. Even the admiring *Time* writer was forced to admit that she often looks as if somebody had thrown her clothes on her as she rushed for a train. She was born Cicily Isabel Fairfield in County

Kerry and began her career as an actress. She took her present name from a part she played in Ibsen's play *Rosmersholm*; she was the unhappy heroine of the piece. She soon turned to writing—novels, literary criticism, and journalism. *The Thinking Reed* and *Black Lamb and Grey Falcon* stand as her major achievements in the world of literature. What her reports on the Republican, Democratic, and Progressive party conventions in Philadelphia can stand for is the question to be examined now.

Miss West arrived in Philadelphia about the time the Republican convention opened, and she began her first article with the statement that it is very hard for the foreigner to understand another country, even with the help of a lifelong affection. For the balance of that session, through the ones held by the Democrats and the Progressives, Miss West attempted to understand America, but the affection quickly got a little strained. The generous human warmth of her womanly nature became ever so slightly chilled, despite the great heat which prevailed in Philadelphia during the conventions.

On June 22 she left all the generous human warmth of a womanly nature in the icebox and cut loose with asperity at the devices which took the proceedings of the convention out of the hall and into the homes of millions of Americans, who do have an interest in knowing what's going on. In more fishwifely prose than she is accustomed to use, Miss West devoted her entire Philadelphia report that day to the thesis that public meetings are being robbed of all effect on those present by the multitude of mechanical devices which are employed to record them for the benefit of people who are not there—that the convention seemed to be run for the benefit of the picture press, the radio, the movies and television, for that monstrous instrument, the microphone, as Miss West called it. She found the loudspeaker system intolerable. The fierce lights of the newsreel and television crews led her to ask if one could imagine Romeo and Juliet playing the balcony scene in dark glasses or Abraham Lincoln making the Gettysburg address in dark glasses?

We would all, Miss West went on, getting worked up, give a great deal to hear Lincoln make the Gettysburg address with his own voice, but no sensible one of us would give a cent to hear him make the speech through a microphone. Let Miss West retire to her eighty-five-acre farm in Buckinghamshire and pitch her radio set into the Great Ouse River; not even to answer the false analogies, the ineffable remarks about listening to the Gettysburg address, the proceedings of a people's meeting belong to all the people, and they are entitled to see and hear as much of it as possible, no matter if those present have to wear dark glasses against the lights and find their sensibilities tortured by the loudspeaker system. As John Crosby wrote in the *Herald Tribune*, the presence of the reporters and the cameras and the microphone is part of the processes of democracy—to permit as many Americans as possible to witness the selection of their president—and to quote him, not everyone has a press pass, Miss West.

One of the risks you run being the sort of subjective reporter Rebecca West is, is that you are likely to accept what is a truth for you and translate it into a universal truth. Miss West found herself extremely uncomfortable in the convention hall, as did every working reporter there who got out on the floor and did his job. Cameramen after news pictures can be very annoying, a radio man with a walkie-talkie gadget who steps on your feet or who runs the contraption into the small of your back is a downright pest, a newspaper reporter who badgers people with questions is a plague, but you submerge the annoyance of the moment into a larger space; just because it is a truth for you that the dignity and effectiveness of a meeting have been lowered because of their presence, it is not necessarily a general truth. Miss West began her lament about modern communications with the statement that it is high time that somebody started thinking seriously about the technique of public meetings. To which it might be retorted that it is high time Rebecca West realized that we live in the present and not in the past and that the wider the spread of information and truth, the more effective information and truth will become.

Those with a taste for parallels will find it interesting to go back to the time when Cicily Isabel Fairfield took the name Rebecca West from the part she played in *Rosmersholm.* In Ibsen's play, Rebecca West was a woman with advanced ideas for her time in the nineteenth century; she brought those ideas to a house which was immersed in traditions of the past, and those traditions ended in tragedy for her. The Rebecca West of Ibsen found that she could not escape the past. It is a curious sidelight that the actress who took that name seems as a writer to prefer the past and its traditions to the present and its possibilities. She thanks God that the English Parliament has so far kept clear of what she calls this monkey business.

At all three conventions, Miss West was able at most times not to let her irritation at the reporting of them get the better of her rather condescending interest in the people themselves, and up to a point, she found them enjoyable to watch. On her arrival at the Republican convention in Philadelphia, she saw people who were tall, forthright, healthy, vigorous, sensible, and competent. She liked a photograph of Governor Dewey feeding hens with a sentimental air as if, she said, he knew of something very kind that each one of them had done.

Photographs of candidates with children she did not find so pleasant. It would be a good thing, she said, if a picture of any candidate for office looking into the face of a child with a tender expression were treated as an indecent photograph and all persons concerned in the production of it were treated with the usual severity. Miss West was gracious about the demonstrations on the floor. That is what they used to do in the Middle Ages when kings and popes were chosen. Miss West was very amusing in her description of a woman at a Stassen reception: broad in the beam, Miss West wrote, emphasizing that breadth by choosing for a dress a print covered with enormous cabbage roses—a hearty being, one of the best-dressed women Miss West ever saw because, when you went around to the front of her, you found that she had a happy and hopeful face, that she had got just the effect she wanted. Almost like a scene described by the *Time* magazine writer when Miss West throws her arm around one of her purebred Jersey cows and murmurs that it is a beautiful, beautiful creature.

But somewhere during the days of heat and strain at the three conventions, Miss West found her pleasure in the observation of people somewhat alloyed, and her final report on the Progressive Party convention aroused considerable comment. It was, she wrote, as unappetizing an assembly as she had ever seen in America, and she underscored that by saying that at the convention there were a number of young people who were very horrible indeed.

There were the ones, she said, who were embryo Babbitts, having their fling before they settled down to safe and narrow lives—stupid young people, too stupid to understand how the world is run. She never saw so many girls with the restless look on their faces that comes of profound insecurity, of consciousness that neither their physical nor mental resources were adequate and that they must create a personality, somehow, by revolt if nothing else turned up. Miss West never saw so many boys with the sullen eyes and dropped chins which mean a brain just good enough to grasp the complexities of life and to realize that it would never be able to master them. In conclusion, Miss West saw the young people as a possible presentation of the students most likely to flunk in 1949. Certainly not the beautiful, beautiful creatures Miss West's Jersey cows are.

Now you can see a variety of faces in America, probably a greater variety than you can in any other land. Some of them may not appeal to one's aesthetic sense since few of them have the placid regularity of a Jersey bossy's features. If Miss West talked to any of the young people she so sweepingly characterizes as horrible and stupid, she does not write about it, and a careful reporter would hesitate to generalize about the caliber of intelligence behind the facade of a face. It might be Steinmetz, it might be Abraham Lincoln, who earlier British writers than Rebecca West thought resembled an ape.

Miss West's story brought immediate reaction from *Herald Tribune* readers, some pro, some con. They wrote about a hundred letters, in the ratio of ten against Miss West, one for, and the *Herald Tribune* printed some of them in that proportion. Mostly, the letters were from adherents of Henry Wallace, who replied strictly on an ideological basis; they felt they had been maligned because of their politics, and that may indeed have influenced Rebecca West. She found the convention distasteful because of the presence of the Communists; it was a truth for her that no young people associated with such a convention could be anything but stupid and horrible. One is entitled to one's own opinion as to the merits or demerits of the Progressive Party's convention and how it was operated. Other reporters than Miss West went into the Communist angle of the convention story, seeing it as prominent or unimportant according to their political opinions or those of the publications for whom they were working. But whatever their politics, whatever their prejudices or personal opinions, the objective ones among them did not pass judgment on the intelligence of those present simply by the look on their faces. They at least made their assessments on the basis of what was said and done. One of those who protested Miss West's article was the novelist Margaret Halsey, who is no Wallace fan but who was quick to point out that a good many Americans of all political faiths would be shocked by Miss West's comments, and she raised the not unnatural question of how Miss West herself looked to the young people.

Did they find her, Miss Halsey asked, the tastiest arrangement of protoplasm their sullen eyes had ever lit upon? Miss Halsey might well have added that even a high-type working reporter, elbowing his way in the 105-degree temperature of Convention

Hall, sweating to get a story, his ribs and feet sore from encounters with the multitude, might not look so intelligent, either—might look, to paraphrase what that *Time* writer said of Miss West herself, as if his clothes had been thrown on him while he was hurrying for a train, and his jaw might be dropping from fatigue. Horrible, in fact, and nothing like as beautiful as a Jersey cow.

To sum up this commentary on the judgment of mentality by faces, one might refer Rebecca West to a couple of politicians for whom she has expressed admiration. To a Republican, Abraham Lincoln, who himself referred to his poor, lean, lank face, and to a Democrat, Woodrow Wilson, whose favorite limerick was one by Anthony Euwer. Wilson liked it because he himself was conscious that he was no beauty. It goes as follows:

As a beauty I'm not a great star,
There are others more handsome by far;
But my face I don't mind it
Because I'm behind it—
'Tis the folks out in front that I jar.

## August 21, 1948

Hollenbeck ruminated in this broadcast about an age-old question for journalists: What kind of news report most effectively moves the reader, listener, or viewer to connect emotionally with a story? He found an answer in a twenty-one-part series by Ray Sprigle of the *Pittsburgh Post-Gazette*, syndicated in the *New York Herald Tribune* and fourteen other U.S. newspapers. Hollenbeck saw Sprigle, a sixty-one-year-old Pulitzer Prize–winning reporter with forty-three years in journalism, as a heroic figure—"a sort of reportorial ideal." To get at the truth, Sprigle was willing to do almost anything. At various times he posed as a coal miner, a psychopathic hospital patient, an illegal gambler, a black-market butcher, and, by blackening his skin and shaving his head, an African American traveling alone through the segregated South. At broadcast's end, Hollenbeck contrasted Sprigle's brand of journalism with that of Rebecca West and an ambulance-racing radio-car photographer for the *New York Mirror*. Hollenbeck left little doubt as to his favorite kind.

ONE OF THE MOST TALKED-ABOUT journalistic events of recent weeks has been the series in the *New York Herald Tribune* entitled "In the Land of Jim Crow"—a series by one of the best reporters in the business, Ray Sprigle of the *Pittsburgh Post-Gazette*. For a month, Sprigle posed as a Negro to find out exactly how some of our people live below what he came to call the "Smith and Wesson Line," and his reports, printed in fifteen American newspapers, none of them in the South, have been the most stimulating and thought-provoking pieces published in the American press in a long time. Many sociologists have written learnedly of the problems of race relations in America; it is safe to say that not one of them has produced one-tenth of the effect Ray Sprigle did by passing as a Negro on a month's four-thousand-mile tour through Georgia, Alabama, Mississippi, and Tennessee. In a very real sense, Reporter Sprigle got into the story with everything he had, and if he doesn't carry off another Pulitzer Prize for his Jim Crow series, these annual awards for excellence in journalism won't have much meaning.

The Jim Crow series illustrated vividly the fact that one story, properly dramatized and brought home to the reader as a vicarious personal experience, is worth volumes of theoretical stuff—also worth volumes of case histories with which the reader can make no personal contact. That was also illustrated by the case of the Russian schoolteachers, as was pointed out the other night by Edward R. Murrow when he said,

> Scenes such as this have been repeated over and over again in Germany, in Spain, in Russia, and in every country where the state has become the custodian of individual rights. But from those happenings we were cushioned by distance, and many of us feel somehow that something that happens far away just doesn't happen at all. But it does: the broken body of a bewildered little Russian schoolteacher lying in a New York courtyard hit us with greater force than reports that dozens have been shot trying to cross a frontier or that another batch of miserable humans are walking the well-beaten trail to Siberia. This is really an old, old story—it just happened here.

So it is with Ray Sprigle's series of articles on Jim Crow. As so many readers of those stories commented, well, we knew these things pretty much all along—he didn't really make any new points. It was simply that by deepening the pigmentation of his skin, Reporter Sprigle was able to bring what is actually an old story into sharper focus—able to give it dimensions into which the reader could fit himself.

It isn't really news that the state of Georgia does not permit Negroes to use a single foot of the state's ocean-bathing beaches, not even in segregated areas. It seems to mean more to hear from Reporter Sprigle that he carried a pair of swim trunks for three thousand miles on his journey through the South, only to find he had no use for them when he reached Savannah and Brunswick. The economic waste of Jim Crow has been pointed out time and again by economists. Reporter Sprigle made it seem more real by actually being forced to use the duplicate facilities which Jim Crow installs for citizens he considers second-rate.

For one month, Ray Sprigle was to all intents and purposes a Negro, and some of the preparations he went through to get his story, and some of the things that happened to him while he was getting it, make a fascinating story in themselves. He'd been wanting to do the Jim Crow story for a long time, and he finally concluded that the only way it could be done properly was to pass the color line. Sprigle was sixty-two years old last Saturday. He's a big man, well fed, and fair—a Dutchman, he calls himself. In order to pass, he had scientists at Pittsburgh's Mellon Institute try to find a dye that wouldn't sweat off and even sent to South America for some mahogany bark.

He tried walnut juice, iodine, Argyrol—nothing worked. Finally, he shaved his head and loafed for three weeks in the sun in Florida. When he was satisfied his deep tan would permit him to pass, he went to Washington and was provided with a Negro guide by Walter White, executive director of the National Association for the Advancement of Colored People. This guide was the only Negro who knew his identity, although he had a close call once in the South; he's naturally a talkative man, and once in a small restaurant, he forgot his resolution to keep reasonably quiet. Later the proprietress said to the guide, "That friend of yours—he talks too much to be a Negro. I think he's white."

The Jim Crow series crowns a career of forty-three years in journalism, during which time Ray Sprigle has turned in story after story to make himself a sort of reportorial ideal. In 1938 he won a Pulitzer Prize for publicizing the Ku Klux Klan membership of Supreme Court Justice Hugo Black. Before that, Sprigle caused a shake-up in the Pittsburgh city administration by disguising himself as a rheumatic cripple and having himself committed to the Pittsburgh Psychopathic Hospital. In 1945 he got the Headliners' Award for public service and touched off a grand jury investigation by posing as a black-market meat operator. But as many times as Ray Sprigle has posed as someone else in order to get a story, he's never had quite the same effect as he has this time, and so thoroughly did he get into the feeling of his story that he found his mind passing the color line, too.

The effectiveness of the Sprigle articles raised one question: Why wouldn't they have been equally effective if done by a Negro journalist, who could have had opportunities for observation and study not available to a white man posing as a Negro? There were no facts in the Sprigle articles which a Negro journalist couldn't have had. In fact, a Negro journalist on the same trip probably would have collected many times the material the *Post-Gazette* reporter did. The reason for the impact of the Sprigle articles would seem to be twofold: First, there was the element of drama. The fact that the reporter had disguised himself as a member of another race added the spice that made the stories more readable; one felt with Sprigle all along that one was running a risk in the adventure. Second, there was no question in the Sprigle articles of self-interest. An outsider making a report on conditions is held to be more objective than one whose interests are closely identified with the subject of the report, providing the reporter approaches that subject with an open mind.

As is always the case with articles of the sort written by Ray Sprigle, their publication inspired a lot of people to write letters to the *Herald Tribune*. About sixty in all, some pro, some con, all violently controversial. On the same day that some of the letters were printed, the *Herald Tribune* ran an editorial on the same page, which seemed to be half-apologetic for the Sprigle articles. It underscored the fact that editors feel they must walk on eggs when so delicate a topic as race relations is under discussion, and in effect, it detracted from the value of the Sprigle articles by pointing out that the North really couldn't point the finger of accusation at the South, which wasn't the point. No editor would need to be even halfway backward about printing the Jim Crow series.

It was mentioned that the outsider can often do a more objective job of reporting on a subject than an insider can, if he approaches his subject with an open mind. And that brings to mind another sample of reporting by the English novelist Rebecca West, particularly interesting when set in contrast with Ray Sprigle's job. A couple of weeks ago, we discussed certain aspects of Miss West's reporting of the national conventions in Philadelphia, reporting done for a syndicate of American and Canadian papers, including the *Herald Tribune.* Miss West did another reporting job at the conventions for newspapers in the United Kingdom, distributed by the Canada Wide syndicate and the *London Evening Standard.* There have come to hand some of the stories Miss West wrote for English readers, and in the light of some of the comments in them, it is little wonder that nations have a hard time understanding each other. For her American readers, Miss West had presumed to pass judgment on the intelligence of those attending the Wallace convention by the way they looked, but for her English, Scottish, and South African readers, she went even farther.

For her United Kingdom readers, Miss West found it possible to generalize even more from practically no information than she had for Americans. Miss West commented on the Negroes' part in the convention in terms which no American editor would find it fair or possible to print; she drew conclusions from personal and hasty observations that no American reporter would have found it possible to draw. For instance, the observation that while the people at the Wallace convention hated England, they hated America more and weren't worth much anyway.

We had intended on this broadcast to give our listeners some samples of Miss West's reporting of the conventions for the English,

Scottish, and South African papers, and under American copyright laws, this would have presented no problem. But permission for CBS to use any part of Miss West's articles written for publication abroad has been flatly forbidden by J. M. Dechene, general manager of Canada Wide Feature Service, which handled the distribution. Any use, Dr. Dechene says, would be considered an infringement. One can see that viewing the press sometimes presents difficulties, but perhaps it's just as well that the planned excerpts from Rebecca West's articles in the *London Evening Standard* have had to be scrapped. The sound of them would have been something of an infringement upon a pleasant Saturday evening.

But it was at the Democratic convention that Miss West did some reporting on conditions among Negroes in the United States that is interesting when set in contrast with Ray Sprigle's series. Miss West was discussing the injection of the civil-rights issue into the convention and at one point gave her English readers the following picture: "The Negroes are now as well fed, housed, clothed, and exercised as they have been since the race came into existence." It would have been helpful if Miss West might have been present a day or two along Ray Sprigle's four-thousand-mile tour.

Ray Sprigle got his story after weeks of slow, patient work over a four-thousand-mile trip, much of it by hitchhiking. It is a good example of dogged work on a reporter's part, and it's the only way a story of this kind can be obtained. But speed is still the objective of the modern newspaper, and more and more gadgets are being perfected to get the news and pictures in practically nothing flat. The *New York Mirror* has a picture automobile that is the last word in gadgetry. It's fitted out with a complete darkroom and, in addition, has a three-thousand-dollar soundfoto transmitting machine which sends photographs by radio direct to the office. We put some CBS recording equipment in Radio Car 2, as they call it, and you'll hear now how *Mirror* photographers go into action to get a picture quickly. Arthur Aidala is the photographer, and we've just heard police signal thirty-two—an accident. Photographer Aidala reaches for the telephone with one hand and starts his car with the other as he calls his office:

**Tape Cue #2**

AIDALA: *Mirror* Radio Car 2, Artie Aidala calling the office—car 2 calling the desk.

VOICE: Yes, Arthur?

AIDALA: We're rolling on a signal thirty-two. Three forty-nine West Fifty-seventh Street, ambulance responding. I'm heading out of Central Park now at Seventy-second Street.

VOICE: All right, Arthur, give me a quick flash when you get there.

AIDALA: I'll do that—car 2 off. (MOTOR NOISE)

HOLLENBECK: And a few minutes later:

AIDALA: I'm only a few blocks away now; I'm pulling out of Central Park South and Seventh Avenue. The address is 349—I imagine between Ninth and Tenth avenues. (HORN SOUND)

HOLLENBECK: The sound of a horn in crowded New York—the sound that speaks louder than words and says, "How do we get through this heavy traffic in time to catch the story and take a picture before the chance is gone?" Aidala explains:

AIDALA: You see, the ambulance responding will be coming from Roosevelt Hospital on Fifty-ninth Street and Tenth Avenue; they're only a few blocks away, so it's really a rat race between the ambulance and myself right now.

HOLLENBECK: In this case, the *Mirror* radio car gets to the scene just in time to get the picture story. Aidala hops out of the car with his gear, learns that a woman has been injured in a one-story fall, shoots the picture, and reports to the desk:

**Tape Cue #3**

AIDALA: . . . third floor, landed on the second-floor roof. She's semiconscious. I got here as they carried her out and made a close-up in the ambulance. She's forty-two, and she's been moved to Roosevelt Hospital.

VOICE: Okay—we see her face in the stretcher, don't we?

AIDALA: Yes, we do, in the close-up.

VOICE: Okay—can you get that stuff in or do you have to clear it?

AIDALA: I can run it right in for you; I'll call you as I near the office building, and you can have an office boy waiting at the door so he can take my holder. Car 2—come in, Tom.

VOICE: That's what I wanted to find out—if we have it exclusive or did someone else get it?

AIDALA: We've got it exclusive, Tom. I got there just as they were carrying out the woman's body. She's still alive, of course.

HOLLENBECK: All this as the *Mirror* radio car heads back to the office, where a messenger is waiting. The film holder handed over, Aidala says:

AIDALA: The boy has gone up. He has the plate, he has the names. Now all you have to do is develop it, and you've got the picture. Any further orders?

VOICE: That'll be all.

HOLLENBECK: Thus is the urge for speed satisfied by science, and a contrast in the manner of covering stories: Ray Sprigle takes four weeks to get a story of Jim Crow in the South, and radio photo cars race ambulances to the scene of an accident.

## September 11, 1948

The opening to this broadcast—about a change in ownership at the weekly *New York Age*—reflected Hollenbeck's desire to report on every aspect of New York media, from the Chinese-language press, to the African American press, to even the *Weekly Block*, a neighborhood paper published by two boys, one ten years old, the other nine. Hollenbeck tried to make the New York press feel that his eyes and ears were open, day and night, to everything. When the *Star* and *Sun* stopped publishing, he interviewed disconsolate reporters at the scene and recorded the papers' last press runs. After he applauded a cleverly written account of flying saucers that appeared in a *Sun* first edition, he received a note from the *Sun* reporter: "You must really be on the ball to spot a feature that runs for one edition."[1] For this broadcast, Hollenbeck created two characters, Mr. and Mrs. George Spavin, to humorously criticize *Journal-American* columnist Westbrook Pegler, who wrote regularly about Mr. and Mrs. George Spelvin, fictional Americans. Pegler was a self-described professional dissenter, published in 174 papers with ten million subscribers, and ranked as the nation's "best adult columnist." He became more shrilly conservative as he aged.[2] He attacked the civil rights movement, espoused anti-Semitism (a position Hollenbeck criticized), and eventually wrote screeds for the John Birch Society's magazine. He earned the label of "the stuck whistle of journalism."[3]

1. "Invisible Man" to Don Hollenbeck, July 16, 1947, in Hollenbeck scrapbook, Don Hollenbeck, Broadcast Papers (MS 319), Archives and Special Collections, University of Nebraska–Lincoln Libraries.
2. David Witwer, "Westbrook Pegler and the Anti-union Movement," *Journal of American History* 92, no. 2 (September 2005): 528.
3. Witwer, "Westbrook Pegler," 527.

September 11, 1948

*CBS VIEWS THE PRESS* would like to take this occasion to welcome a new publisher to the New York newspaper field. His name is Richard Bourne-Vanneck, he's an Englishman, and the newspaper of which he's the new publisher is the *New York Age*, one of the country's oldest Negro newspapers. Before we tell you about Bourne-Vanneck's interesting new plans for the *Age*, we'd like to tell you something about the man himself. You see, Bourne-Vanneck happens to be white, and we say "happens to be" because he finds nothing either odd or unusual about the fact that he has just bought a Negro newspaper or the fact that his wife is a Negro. In fact, he is likely to get somewhat excitable about people who do think it's unusual, and that's all part of the story. In his native England, Bourne-Vanneck was an engineer. He worked for a long time with Americans and in an American firm, and he always wanted to come to America to get into business. In 1940, at a university dance at Cambridge, he met Victoria Thomas. Miss Thomas had been born in England of Negro parents, had been taken to the United States at the age of two, and brought back to England at the age of thirteen to complete her education. Bourne-Vanneck and Miss Thomas were mightily attracted to each other, and in 1943 they married.

That solidified Bourne-Vanneck's determination to get to the United States, which he finally did eight months ago after selling out his interest in an engineering combine. In buying the *Age*, Bourne-Vanneck doesn't see himself doing anything as melodramatic as throwing in his lot with the Negro people and fighting their battles, and in fact he seems somewhat taken aback at the suggestion. So far as he's concerned, he says, this doesn't mean any radical change in his life, except that now he's a newspaper publisher instead of a businessman. He picks his friends as he always did, without any regard for their color, and his business associates the same way. He says that before buying the *Age*, he and his wife considered quite a few other business propositions, but this one simply seemed like the best one. Bourne-Vanneck is a youngish man, and from his appearance one would judge that the addition of forty years to his age might make him look something like the famed caricature of Colonel Blimp. So far as his intellect is concerned, nothing could be more deceiving. His plans for the *Age* are, in terms of Negro journalism and perhaps of white journalism, too, radical. To help him carry them out, he has employed one of the best Negro newspapermen in the business: Dan Burley, columnist and managing editor of the *Amsterdam News*. Together, they explained to us what's going to happen if their plans materialize. Very soon, the new *Age* will hit the newsstands. Thereafter it will come out every Friday and Tuesday: twenty standard-sized pages on Friday looking somewhat like the *World-Telegram*, forty tabloid pages on Tuesday looking somewhat like the *Daily News*.

Whichever format is more successful will continue permanently when they start publishing as a daily newspaper, which will be as soon as possible. As to content, Bourne-Vanneck and Burley give us this bit of background. They feel that the Negro press in the United States grew up during a time when every moment counted in the fight for economic and political existence. As a result, they feel that the Negro press has, perhaps, been too much propaganda and not enough newspaper. But, they say, tremendous strides have been made during the past few years, especially in New York. The time has come when people should participate in the community not as Negroes but as Americans. The motto on the masthead of the new *Age* will be: "In all things we stand together as Americans." They say they are going to make the *Age* a newspaper whose primary service area is uptown Manhattan, holding somewhat the same place in the community as the old *Bronx Home News*. Since uptown Manhattan is largely Negro, naturally the *Age* will contain a lot of Negro news, not only local but national and international since, as Bourne-Vanneck says, "The Negroes still have a special national and international community of interest." However, Mr. Burley, who will be in active charge of the editorial departments, says that "we are not going to segregate ourselves as to news." If there is a marriage of a prominent uptown citizen who happens not to be Negro, that will be duly reported with no to-do made of the fact that he is white.

When the *Age* becomes a daily newspaper, it will probably contain the full national and international coverage of the United Press, just like any other newspaper. In other words, Bourne-Vanneck and Burley hope to make it into a newspaper out of which the uptown citizenry can get a full budget of the day's events without having to buy another newspaper. As to their handling of race problems, they plan no emphasis on the sordid, such as riot and crime, but rather on the positive elements of race relations that point the way for a better future. Burley says they may flounder for a while but not for long because they know just exactly what they're going to do. They're gathering a staff together now, and it will be one of the few in the country with both whites and Negroes on the editorial side. So far, two white men have been hired. Politically, the *Age* will be independent.

Now, all this is not to say that the *Age* will be a wishy-washy, fence-sitting newspaper. Perhaps we can give you its basic attitude best by quoting a paragraph from an editorial by Henry Lee Moon, which will appear in that first new edition:

> The new *Age* makes no pretense to a spurious objectivity. We confess to a bias. We are against bigotry in any form. We are against those who preach and practice race hatred. We are against those who would erect false barriers between man and man. We are against those who deny the basic equality of all men. We are against those who would appease the false enemies of mankind. We are for full recognition of the Negro American's citizenship. We are for those forces which are working for a society of peace, equality, and justice

for all. We do not believe that the lyncher is entitled to the same consideration as his victim.

The fictional characters George and Mary Spelvin, Americans, have been taken over from the theater by Westbrook Pegler, and in their living room in Dudgeon Heights, the Spelvins talk about a variety of things every week in the supplement of the *Journal-American*. For purposes of parallel, we'd like to imagine this afternoon that we are Mr. and Mrs. George Spavin, also Americans, and that we are sitting around our living room in Fantastic Flats. We're going to talk about the recent attack by Westbrook Pegler on Bert Andrews of the *Herald Tribune*, and as the Spavin discussion develops, some misconceptions may be cleared up. I'm going to play the part of George Spavin—I think I'm an American—and the part of Mary Spavin will be taken by Julie Bennett, an American actress employed by CBS News for this occasion. Miss Bennett, as Mary Spavin, opens the conversation:

MARY: Well, they've finally caught up to that fellow Bert Andrews of the *Herald Tribune*, haven't they?

GEORGE: You mean the Bert Andrews who won himself a Pulitzer Prize awhile back for his stories about how they took away the civil liberties of some guys working for the State Department—tried to fire them without telling them why or giving them a chance to defend themselves?

MARY: I guess so. Anyway, this Andrews has written a book about it called *Washington Witch Hunt*, and oh boy, does old Peg ever take him apart! He gives you the idea Andrews is no good as a reporter, and not only *Andrews* either; I guess from what Peg says there can't be a good reporter working in Washington any more. In his column the other day, Peg was talking about the journalistic standards down there these days. He said that by a miracle of laziness, venality, and stupidity so gross as to jeopardize the future of a free press, the standards have been even worse in the sixteen years of Roosevelt and Truman than they were in the twenties.

GEORGE: That sounds like Peg, all right—he can sure make with the words. But look, Mary, that means the whole bunch of reporters down there in Washington are lazy, stupid, and what was that other word? Venality? What does that mean, Mary?

MARY: I looked it up in Webster and copied it down; it says, "open to corrupt influence or bribery." Golly, I guess old Peg is just about the last *honest* reporter left in America, isn't he?

GEORGE: Guess so—but think of it, Mary! All the newspapers who have their own reporters in Washington or who use the press association copy from there and use Pegler's column, too—there's about three hundred of those papers—they're guilty of defrauding the public if Peg's right, and they ought to do something about it.

MARY: But about that book—*Washington Witch Hunt.* Peg says it's a terrible worriment over the tenuous possibility that some person might be falsely accused by personal enemies and dismissed from a job in the government. Yes, George, I looked up "tenuous," too. It means having slight support or basis.

GEORGE: I'm not sure just what Peg means there. You'd think from that that none of these things happened, but those guys in the State Department actually did have a pretty rough time, as I remember it. Wasn't that why Bert Andrews won his Pulitzer Prize? For telling what happened?

MARY: Well, that's the way I thought it was, but reading Pegler, I'm sort of mixed up. But, George, listen to this—it sounds pretty sinister to me. Peg says, "Finally, after an interesting crusade of intimidation against the committee which confers the Pulitzer awards, Mr. Andrews received the capital prize of the profession." What does he mean by "intimidation," George? Did Andrews say, "Look, you guys better give me a Pulitzer Prize, or else?"

GEORGE: Well, Peg doesn't exactly SAY that, but you might get that impression; he doesn't make it very clear just who did the intimidating. Those Pulitzer guys are a lot of big shots: Frank Kent of the *Baltimore Sun*, Arthur Krock of the *New York Times*, Kent Cooper of the Associated Press, John S. Knight—he owns a couple of newspapers. Oh yes, Joseph Pulitzer, too, of the *St. Louis Post-Dispatch*—his dad started the prizes. I don't think any of those gents would be intimidated by Bert Andrews or by anybody else, and I can't think of a newspaperman with a brain in his head thinking he could browbeat any of those people, can you, Mary?

MARY: No, but anyhow, you've got to admit that Peg sure can sling the words around. Like this: "This job presents the whole whining, reptilian case of the sneak in government who arouses fair suspicions and then, like so many of the witnesses hailed before the committee, instead of *helping* his government to put *down* an alien treachery, defies an ill-equipped congressional committee to prove a case according to the most stilted *jur*idical principles." Ain't that grand, George? Why don't you try writing?

GEORGE: It sure is something, Mary, but wait a minute. None of those people involved in the case Andrews was writing about ever got a chance to go before any committee, even though they asked time and again to tell their stories until the State Department got embarrassed and backed down and let them resign.

GEORGE (Cont'd): Why, Mary, most of those guys don't know to this very day why they were fired in the first place or what the specific charges against them were, and they've never had a chance to defend themselves. But you know, Peg doesn't hold with all those trials and hearings, anyway. He says these guys just clam up and won't talk, and it's just a waste of the taxpayer's money summonsing them and all like that. He says unions fire people like that, too, and he's been slugging that out for years.

MARY: Well, anyhow, Peg says Andrews's book was lavishly praised by the Communist press, and that *ain't* good, is it, George?

GEORGE: That ain't good, Mary. But the only Communist press

I heard about that even reviewed the book was the *Daily Worker*, and it certainly didn't go overboard for it. As I heard it, about half the *Worker*'s review knocked Andrews's brain out. Those Commies get just as het up as Peg does sometimes. All in all, there were about a hundred reviews of Andrews's book in publications like the *New York Times*, the *Christian Science Monitor*, *Newsweek*, and, oh, a lot of publications like that I've never heard of following the party line; most of them liked the book, and they seemed to think Andrews had the right idea. It's a pretty awful thing if the guy's subversive and if he's fooled all those smart apples.

MARY: But, George, the *New York Times* and the *Monitor* and *Newsweek* and people like Kent Cooper and Arthur Krock—it looks as if *they* thought Andrews was *okay*, so why is Peg mad at him? What's it all about anyway?

GEORGE: Darned if I know, Mary. But sometimes I wish old Peg wouldn't worry so much and that he'd report a baseball game now and then. He and Heywood Broun were about the best I remember in the old days.

## October 30, 1948

Hollenbeck repeatedly examined whether the editorial views of New York City's newspapers colored their news coverage. In one broadcast, he reported that the papers opposing a referendum to repeal proportional representation in city-council elections gave ten times as much space in their news columns to reports in favor of proportional representation as did those papers against it. In this broadcast, he looked at coverage of an important national issue. He examined editorial support versus the quantity of news reports in New York City's papers for the four major presidential candidates in 1948. More than two-thirds of America's daily newspapers supported the Republican candidate, New York governor Thomas E. Dewey. Among New York City's dailies, the percentage of editorial support for Dewey was even higher. Interestingly, Hollenbeck's foot-rule survey suggested that—at least in terms of Dewey versus President Harry S. Truman, the Democratic candidate, who would narrowly win—coverage was much more evenhanded than it had been in reporting the referendum to repeal proportional representation.

AS IT HAS BEEN for the past twelve years, the American press this year has been preponderantly in favor of the Republican candidate for the presidency of the United States. A little more than a month ago, a survey by the newspaper trade publication *Editor & Publisher* showed that Governor Dewey was backed by 68 percent of the nation's dailies, President Truman by 16 percent, with the balance of the press supporting either Henry Wallace's Progressive Party or the states'-righters headed by J. Strom Thurmond. Ten percent of the newspapers at the time the poll was taken were undecided or avowed independent, but since that survey was made, Governor Dewey has increased his percentage of newspaper support.

The national proportion doesn't quite apply to New York City. Here President Truman has been given the editorial support of only the *New York Star*, which has the smallest circulation of the nine major dailies in the city. All the others, with the exception of the *Post*, have been solidly behind Governor Dewey, and the *Post* this election year presents something of a journalistic phenomenon—a sort of editorial split personality, if that term may be used in reference to an internal division at the *Post*, as to just whom it does want for president of the United States. The editorial policy of the *Post* is theoretically arrived at after agreement between its editors and publishers, who are Mr. and Mrs. Ted Thackrey—both act in equal capacity in both jobs.

Mr. Thackrey has declared himself in favor of the election of Henry Wallace, but Mrs. Thackrey, after considerable thought, has decided that she is for the election of Governor Dewey, and she says so in an editorial in the weekend edition of the *Post* which went on sale today. Mrs. Thackrey's reasoning is that a Republican will make a better president than an incompetent and inconsistent Democrat (Truman); than a perhaps well-intentioned but pathetically confused and gullible radical (Wallace); than a sincere but pacifistic rather than peace-minded Socialist ([Norman] Thomas). And, Mrs. Thackrey says, a vote for nobody is a vote thrown away. The Thackreys have carried on their political differences of opinion in print over a considerable period of time, but this must be the first time in history that two editors of the same newspaper have been at such polar extremes in their choices of candidates. *Post* readers may be excused if they are somewhat bewildered.

Bearing in mind that newspapers take one side or another in a political campaign in their editorial columns, the question then arises: What do they do in their news columns? Does that perfectly justified editorial one-sidedness show up in what are expected to be factual, unopinionated reports of the comings and goings and sayings of the various candidates? In an effort to find out how the local press reported the three major candidates—President Truman, Governor Dewey, and Henry A. Wallace—*CBS Views the Press* made a detailed study of the newspapers for a limited period: the first two weeks in October, during which the campaign might be said to be approaching its climax.

Our study included the final editions of the morning papers and the first editions of the afternoon papers. We measured the amount of space allotted to the candidates' speeches and activities, the editorials for or against them, and a box score on how the various columnists lined up. News space allotted to polls and surveys of trends were not counted as news stories. Studying the press with a foot-rule is admittedly not the most scholarly method of criticism, but in this case, the foot-rule system did produce some interesting results when assessed in relation to the editorial policy of the newspapers and the performance of their columnists.

Normally, the president of the United States will command more news space than any other American citizen simply by virtue of his preeminent position, but when there's a political campaign on, his opponent theoretically should get equal linage so far as the actual campaign is concerned. Our test of that point centered on the two New York newspapers which might have been expected to ratify the foregone conclusion, but actually it didn't quite work out that way. Although both the *New York Times* and the *Herald Tribune* are editorially for Governor Dewey, they gave the edge on news space to President Truman during the two-week measuring period. The reason for that might have been that the president was slugging a lot harder than Governor Dewey was, and it's an old theory in the newspaper business that an attack is always more newsworthy than a more static statement. Over the period of the entire campaign, the slight news edge given the president might have been equalized, but the period selected seemed for purposes of comparison to be a reasonable one. Editorially, the *Times* was critical of President Truman twice and praised his administration once during the fourteen days; that praise, incidentally, might be considered just a mite two-edged: the *Times* liked the idea that the administration's "Voice of America" was impartial enough to tell the world that Governor Dewey was leading President Truman in the drive for the votes of the American electorate.

During the two-week period, the *Times* printed two editorials favorable to Governor Dewey: one when it came out for his election and again in approving a New York speech he made on housing. The *Times* mentioned Wallace only once editorially, and that was a factual comment on New York City registration figures. The *Herald Tribune* in two weeks had six editorials favorable to Governor Dewey and three critical of President Truman. One comment—adverse—was made on Wallace.

The Truman edge on news reporting was also evident in two other morning newspapers even more outspoken in their editorial support of Governor Dewey—the *News* and the *Mirror*. Again it seemed that by the nature of his campaign and the fact that he was still the president of the United States, Mr. Truman was able to get a bit more linage in the news columns, even though the management of the *News* and *Mirror* will be very unhappy if next Wednesday morning he is declared elected the president of the United States. The *Mirror*, however, gave quite a lot more space to Governor Dewey than the *News* did, and as for Henry Wallace, the *News* was surprisingly generous. Of the total amount of news space devoted to the three candidates, Wallace took about one-seventh, almost as much as the *Herald Tribune* gave him, with much more available space, and in addition, the *News* announced it was giving equal space on its quadrennial presidential battle page to the Progressive Party. The *Mirror* scarcely even bothered to mention the Wallace candidacy. Editorially, the *News* socked Truman three times, endorsed Dewey three times, sniffed at Wallace once. Its star political columnist, John O'Donnell, wrote six columns critical of President Truman and the late President Roosevelt but said nothing positive about Dewey. The *Mirror* shrilled at Truman five times in the two-week period, was nice to Dewey three times, and completely ignored Wallace.

The *New York Star* gave President Truman a slight edge in the news columns over Dewey—remember, the *Star* is the only morning paper supporting the president—but it also considered the Progressive Party important enough news to give Wallace nearly equal space with the other two candidates. Although none of the *Star*'s columnists felt friendly to Dewey, they couldn't agree on the others: Max Lerner turned them down for Norman Thomas, I. F. Stone was critical of Truman twice and favorable to Wallace once.

In the afternoon field, it was almost all Dewey. The *Sun*, the *World-Telegram*, and the *American* all gave the governor a better break in their news columns—the *Sun* printing more than twice as much for its favorite than it did for Truman. So far as the *Sun* was concerned, Henry Wallace might as well not have been running, except for raps by columnists Sokolsky and Lawrence, and on its editorial page; the actual news of the Wallace candidacy constituted one-twenty-eighth of the *Sun*'s political coverage. The *World-Telegram* was consistently fair in its first-page summary of the doings and sayings of the candidates, but in general, Governor Dewey got about a third again as much space as President Truman did. Editorially, the *World-Telegram* was the most vigorous for Dewey in the afternoon field, but its columnists stayed pretty much out of the fracas.

The *Journal-American* comparatively gave more space to President Truman than the *World-Telegram* did, but again, Henry Wallace might as well have stood in bed so far as coverage of his campaign was concerned. Column-wise, George Rothwell Brown carried the ball against Wallace, Westbrook Pegler took on Truman three times. The split-personality problem at the *Post* was illustrated in its news columns for the two-week period: although coeditor Ted Thackrey has declared personally for Henry Wallace, and coeditor Dorothy Thackrey is for Dewey, the paper gave far more space to President Truman than it did to either Dewey or Wallace, and with few exceptions, its many columnists usually wrote pieces critical of the candidates when they wrote about them at all. In the *Post*, you get your politics well scrambled.

Pictorially, both President Truman and Governor Dewey fared equally well as to the number of photographs published during the two weeks—thirty-nine each, by our count, although when you break that down into performances by individual newspapers, it's something else. In fourteen days, the *Mirror* printed twelve pictures of Governor Dewey as against five of President Truman. Henry Wallace wasn't even in the running pictorially; not a single photograph appeared in the editions we checked, but it must be remembered that, during this period, nobody was throwing eggs and tomatoes at the Progressive Party candidate.

The Progressive Party generally fared very badly as to press coverage during the period of measurement; of the nearly 5,700 total column inches devoted to reporting on the presidential candidates, Wallace got one-ninth. The main complaint of the Wallace publicity people, though, was not about overall press coverage—they didn't seem to expect much more than they got. But they did feel bitter about what they said was the rush of the press to make hay out of possible defections from the party and its inclination to ignore the fact that prominent people had come out for Wallace. They complained that no mention had been made of the fact that such people as Thomas Mann, Pierre Van Paasen, and Frank Lloyd Wright had endorsed Wallace, but in that connection, the Republicans might have a complaint, too: Lionel Barrymore, Louis Bromfield, and Raymond Moley came out for Dewey, but so far as we could find, that didn't seem to be news so far as the newspapers were concerned.

As one editor said, "Every night, we cart bushels and bushels of press releases out of the city room. We'd be glad to print a lot of that stuff if the people who are putting it out could arrange to furnish us with several extra tons of newsprint every day." The editor's lament is understandable. The output of political press agents in presidential years must gladden the hearts of those who hold stock in mimeograph-machine companies, and the deficit in the Post Office Department must be considerably lightened.

One public figure who became important politically was Joe Louis, but there was considerable confusion in the press as to just how he figured. As a columnist for the *New York Age*, Louis appeared at Grand Central Station to see Dewey off on one of his campaign trips. That much the reporters could agree on, but they were at odds otherwise: the *Mirror* said that Louis joined the supporters of Governor Dewey, as he had four years ago. The *Times* said the champion wouldn't indicate whom he was supporting. The Associated Press and United Press were split; the former said Louis told reporters he'd support Dewey, the latter said he dodged the question. The *Tribune* took no chances—it simply said that the governor was suffering from bursitis in his right arm, therefore extended his left in greeting to the boxer. As for exactly what happened, Billy Roe of Louis's staff said the *Times* was nearest right, and he added that since Louis was about to start on a tour, it would be silly to get involved in any partisan discussion that might affect the box office. But he did add that Louis himself is going to vote for Governor Dewey.

The campaign hasn't been notable for any particular journalistic achievement—after all, you can do just so much with the speeches and public appearances of political candidates—but the *New York Times* did get out of the rut once, and somewhat surprisingly. It was when the newspaper's James B. Reston was accompanying the Dewey special west, and from Claremore, Oklahoma, Reston turned in a piece to make one wonder how it ever got past the *Times*'s very proper copydesk. Describing how Governor Dewey said farewell to the crowds at whistle-stops, the concluding paragraph of Reston's story concludes, "'Good-bye, everybody,' the governor shouts, 'good-bye,' and the 'victory special' pulls out—usually with a jerk." The joke has long been in the Joe Miller class of very tired gags, but to see it in the prim *Times* is rather like hearing an off-color joke told by a maiden aunt.

Much funnier was the *Nation*'s ichthyological view of the three candidates—the one bit of really sharp humor we caught during the entire campaign. Ichthyologically, the *Nation*'s cartoonist Oscar Berger and editor Robert Endiner saw the candidates as follows: "*Missouri Weakfish*—Propels itself in short, jerky movements in any direction. Swallows twice its capacity to digest. Gregarious but prefers society of other Missouri Weakfish. *Hudson River Eel*—This elusive creature is highly sensitive and gives off sparks when touched. Has powerful instinctive drive toward the waters of the Potomac River. Travels alone, having had trouble with schools. *Progressive Butterfish*—Member of the croaker family. Changes shape unpredictably. Feeds on Black Sea caviar, apparently without knowing what he is eating. Travels upstream to lay eggs on public platforms."

Well, the campaign fishing trip is about over, and by Wednesday morning, voters will know what the catch is.

## November 13, 1948

If there is one image that has come to symbolize the press's role in the 1948 election, it is a photo of President Harry S. Truman gleefully holding up an early edition of the *Chicago Daily Tribune* that carries a most inaccurate headline: "Dewey Defeats Truman." The coverage of the press was seriously wrong in more than its political prognostication. In this broadcast, Hollenbeck reported on press introspection after Truman's surprise victory. Reporters relied too much on political polls and needed to spend more time at shoe-leather reporting that got them closer to the grass roots. But Hollenbeck went deeper, reflecting on the loss of newspaper circulation, the inability of reporters to connect to the people, and other trends especially relevant today as newspapers fight for survival in the digital age.

IT COULD BE THAT the best thing that ever happened to the American press was what *Time* magazine (including itself in the indictment) has called its appalling election performance, the magazine taking for its text an appropriate quotation from the book of Job: "Is there iniquity in my tongue? Cannot my taste discern perverse things? . . . Teach me, and I will hold my tongue, and cause me to understand wherein I have erred." It could be that the best thing that ever happened to the American press was the humiliating experience it underwent on November 2, but reflection and observation in the eleven days that have passed since the election give cause for wonder if the American press has learned anything from its lesson beyond the simple fact that it was monstrously wrong. If the press *has* been taught wherein it has erred, has it then learned what it must do in the future to see that it reports somewhat more exactly what the American people think and want?

A few newspapermen around the country have learned wherein they erred and why but not many. Notable among them is James Reston of the *New York Times*, one of the country's top reporters, who, on the day after the election, wrote a letter to his editor. The letter was printed in the column reserved for letters to the editor, and even in the newspaper business itself, it received little attention. It might well have been printed on the front pages of every newspaper in the land and within black mourning borders, too—the traditional display with which the press marks the occasion of a great national loss. In this case, the black borders might have been used to announce the fact that the American press seemed to have lost all contact with the people for whom it is published. In his letter, Mr. Reston said, "Before we in the newspaper business spend all our time and energy analyzing Governor Dewey's failure in the election, we ought to try to analyze our own failure. For that failure is almost as spectacular as the president's victory, and the quicker we admit it the better off we'll be. There were certain factors in this election," Mr. Reston goes on, "that were known (and discounted) by almost every political reporter. We knew about the tradition that a defeated candidate had never been nominated and elected after his defeat. We knew that the national income was running at the rate of $210 billion a year, that over sixty-one million persons were employed at unprecedentedly high wages, and that the people had seldom, if ever, turned against the administration in power at such a time."

And then Mr. Reston gets to the real point in his letter to his editor when he says that although political reporters knew all these things, all of them were carried away by facts they did not verify, by theories they did not fully examine, and by assumptions they did not or could not check. Just as politicians had been too isolated with other politicians to know what was really happening, the reporters were too isolated with other reporters, too impressed by the tidy statistics of the polls. Not enough time was spent talking to the people; the reporters tended to assume that somebody else was doing the original reporting in an area. He concludes his letter by saying, "The great intangible of this election was the political influence of the Roosevelt era on the thinking of the nation. It was less dramatic than the antics of Messrs. Wallace and Thurmond, but in the long run, it was more important, and we didn't give enough weight to it. Consequently, we were wrong, not only on the election but, what's worse, on the whole political direction of our time."

That is the point of view of one American newspaperman on the part played by the press in the election. It indicates that he has read the lesson well and that he has been taught to understand wherein he has erred; the question is how generally in the newspaper profession has the lesson been learned and what its intentions are for the future. Another veteran newspaperman, Roy Roberts of the *Kansas City Star*, says the meaning is clear: newspapers must pay more attention to basic facts—get down to grass roots and the lower east side—with hard-boiled reporters searching for changes in mass thinking. Mr. Roberts adds that, while it is the prime function of a newspaper to lead, not to follow, he has come to the conclusion that the newspaper serves its purpose more effectively by setting forth the facts and letting the public make up its own mind rather than for the paper to overstress its own conclusions and expect the public to accept its opinions.

Perhaps Roy Roberts and James Reston and others who caught the significance of the press's failure to keep up with public thinking may cause some changes for the better in the future, but there are also some indications that the realization has not been complete that, as *Time* puts it, the press was morally guilty on several counts. It was guilty of pride: it had assumed that it knew all the important facts without sufficiently checking them. It was guilty of laziness and wishful thinking: it had failed to do its own doorbell ringing and bush beating; it had delegated the journalists' job to the pollsters.

One of the indications that the press as a whole hasn't read the lesson well is in the postelection reflections by *Editor & Publisher*, the trade paper of journalism; it has presumably been speaking for editors and publishers for sixty years. In the same issue it printed Mr. Reston's letter, in its editorial musings on the big upset, the magazine noted that again, as in 1936, 1940, and 1944, the Democratic presidential candidate won the election in the face of majority support for his Republican rival. And once again, it went on, the skeptics, the critics, and even the man in the street are mumbling that the newspapers don't reflect the interests of their readers and that you can't believe what you read in the newspapers. And then by some very ingenious use of figures, the publication endeavors to answer its critics by breaking down newspaper attitudes toward the candidates locally. In other words, in Alabama, Louisiana, Mississippi, and South Carolina, most of the newspapers supported the candidacy of Governor J. Strom Thurmond, and he won the electoral votes of those states. Similarly, Governor Dewey was supported by the majority of the newspapers in the states he carried; so was President Truman in the states which went into his column. Therefore, *Editor & Publisher* concludes, since we do not have a national press, since newspapers wield their influence locally rather than nationally, and since presidents are elected by the total vote of the states instead of by a national vote, the newspapers were right locally after all, and in the concluding words of the editorial, "From these comparisons, it may be seen that any criticism of the daily newspapers on a national basis because of the election results is unfounded." This would seem to establish a new high point in casuistry, and it might seem comic except that it reflects all too clearly the fact that, while the newspapers of the country may individually confess themselves to have been made monkeys of by the voters, the basic thinking of American journalism hasn't changed much, if *Editor & Publisher* represents that thinking, as it has supposedly done for so many years.

November 13, 1948

When *Editor & Publisher* says we do not have a national press, it is playing with words. We do not have a national press in the sense that England does—a very few newspapers with country-wide circulation—but as a matter of fact, the American press as a whole is as nearly a national press as could be imagined. The steady decline in the number of newspapers, the concentration of newspaper ownership in the hands of a comparatively few powerful persons, their community of interest as a big business, the increasing use of syndicated material, the growth of publicity handouts to the proportions of a national industry—all these things have tended to give the American press a uniformity to the point that, in the main, one newspaper is very like another. You read the same syndicated features in them all, and there has been a notable decline in vigorous individual journalism. As Edward R. Murrow pointed out the other night, ours is a highly mechanized country, our clothes are largely standardized, we tell pretty much the same stories, use the well-advertised goods of mass production. Much of our information is mass-produced, superimposed on the country by syndicated columns written in New York or Washington or by broadcasts originating in those two cities.

The results of the election have presented a real challenge to all media of information in America, and again, the question is whether the challenge will be met with the failure to rely so much on ready-made and secondhand opinion or if, as *Editor & Publisher* indicates, the newspapers have really nothing to be ashamed of after all. Mechanization is difficult to scrap once you've got used to it. It's so much easier to print the opinions of a well-publicized expert a thousand miles away than it is to get out and try to get the facts for yourself, and the operation and production of American newspapers have been becoming more and more mechanized in all departments to the point that a body of them claiming nearly 80 percent of the readers of the nation joined in a failure for the fifth consecutive presidential election to realize what the American people wanted and what they were doing about it.

Part of these reflections and observations are based on a visit by this reporter to Chicago this week, the occasion being the annual meeting of the Associated Press Managing Editors Association. About three hundred managing editors were present from around the country to discuss with Associated Press executives ways and means of improving the newspapers and the news report of the Associated Press. As one of the association's study committees put it, "The whole aim of this effort is making newspapers more useful to their readers and creating a better-informed public. What the reader wants in a news story is the essential facts plus sufficient explanatory matter to enable him to place the particular event in its true perspective and to evaluate its significance and importance."

Politics was naturally one of the engrossing topics at this year's session. Gathered there at the Drake Hotel were some of the top men of the newspaper business—editors charged with the responsibility of leadership in their community and with making, as the committee put it, newspapers more useful to their readers and with creating a better-informed public. One of the sessions was turned over to discussion of the election coverage; the editors were very sensible of the fact that, in most cases, they had failed to measure the temper and the trend in their communities and that, even far into the election night, there was a lack of realization as to what was happening. The discussion brought out the interesting fact that the Associated Press, as the night wore on and the returns kept piling up, had attempted to get from its member newspapers around the country a guess as to what was going on—what the opinion of the editors was as to the outcome. Nothing, it turned out, was developed which was of any use—no editors even late that night would get themselves out on a limb so far as to guess what their communities were doing. The preconception as to the election's outcome had so far paralyzed them as to make them unable to shift ground even at the eleventh hour and to realize how blindly wrong they had been.

In the open discussion, at least, the basic reasons for the error were brushed over, but at one point late in the talk, a young managing editor from the Southwest made an interesting point. He had been misled like all the rest, but he said that early on election night, he got a comment from an employee. Not an editorial writer or a reporter or a political expert on his newspaper. The comment was made to him by the night watchman, and it took the form of an accurate prediction as to what was happening. The watchman said, "You know, the trouble with you newspapermen is that you talk to the wrong people; if you'd get out and around the right places enough, you'd know what was going on." That is another and simpler way of saying what James Reston and Roy Roberts said, and it would seem to be the very crux of this entire question of how the press went so wrong on this election. But the young man from the Southwest sparked no argument among the editors with his observation; he was just a young managing editor after all and from rather a small paper. But a thorough-going threshing out of that particular point might result in a complete change of the American press—a determination to get around and see the right people. It would take a lot of legwork, but it would be worth it.

For as it is now, on the basis of its election performance, the American press in the larger view stands convicted of what the book of Job calls iniquity in its tongue, with taste unable to discern perverse things. It stands now neither as the leader of public opinion nor a follower; it couldn't influence the people to vote the way it thought they ought to vote, and it couldn't find out what the people were thinking, even though, as James Reston says, all the facts and factors were available to it all the time. It kept looking into the faces of the people and seeing only itself.

## July 9, 1949

Hollenbeck devoted large chunks of three broadcasts to coverage of the controversial case of liberal icon Alger Hiss, a former State Department official. Whittaker Chambers, a *Time* senior editor, had accused Hiss of passing government secrets to the Soviets. While A. J. Liebling, writing for the *New Yorker*, and other commentators depicted Hiss as a lamb being led to journalistic slaughter, Hollenbeck avoided portraying Hiss as a wronged innocent. Hiss said that Hollenbeck was, "if not unique, certainly extremely unusual in his objectivity and his fairness . . . and courage. It took courage to be fair then."[1] Out of fairness and caution, Hollenbeck asked Joseph Wershba, then a CBS correspondent in Washington, to contact Bert Andrews of the *Herald Tribune*, an expert on the Hiss-Chambers case. Andrews told Wershba, "Look, you better tell Don, 'Be careful with this thing. There's a lot that Chambers knows about Hiss.'"[2] While Hollenbeck was careful in this broadcast about Hiss's first perjury trial in 1949, he did not refrain from reviewing newspaper articles and headlines for imbalance and overstatement.

DURING THE TRIAL of Alger Hiss for perjury, just concluded inconclusively, federal judge Samuel H. Kaufman made a comment which seems worthy to serve as the text for today's discussion. About a month after the trial had been in progress, Judge Kaufman made the following observation: "It has been called to my attention that there have been various columnists writing about their views of the case, some of whom have been in court and some of whom have not been here. It is unfortunate that that

1. Alger Hiss, interview with editor, June 16, 1975, New York. Hiss cited Hollenbeck's coverage of his first trial in *In the Court of Public Opinion* (New York: Alfred A. Knopf, 1957), 297–98.
2. Joseph Wershba, interview with editor, November 10, 1974, New Hyde Park NY.

kind of thing can take place with respect to an important case of this kind, but it is taking place. What the court can do about it, I do not know, but after the conclusion of this trial, the subject should be considered either by the court or through some other method." And Judge Kaufman went on, "This jury should not be influenced by outside sources. I have attempted to indicate to the jury that they have taken an oath at the commencement of this trial to try the case on the evidence as it is adduced in the courtroom without regard to what they see or hear outside. That is not evidence, and if we are going to get trials by publicity, the function of the courts will end." That statement was displayed prominently only in the *Times*, and we'll deal in a moment or two with the specific matter Judge Kaufman was discussing. But his remarks will also serve us as a point of departure for some general remarks about how the metropolitan press behaved during the six weeks Alger Hiss was on trial.

We might open with the general observation that it's a good thing the jury of ten men and two women weren't obliged to reach their decision on the basis of what they read in the newspapers because if they had, an already complex case would have been rendered downright incomprehensible to them. A trial of the proportions of the Alger Hiss affair offers a tremendous challenge to reporters and editors—who should at all times attempt to keep a balance—to present, along with rapidly developing events, enough background or explanatory material to provide fair perspective. In the Hiss case, we had nearly a million words of testimony offered and more thousands of words of oratory by opposing counsel. Let's see how this tremendous outpouring of the English language was funneled through the columns of the metropolitan newspapers to their readers.

We can take as an example the afternoon of June 24, which was the second day Alger Hiss was called as a witness in his own defense. One of the main points of his testimony was that he stood by his own story that the last time he had seen Whittaker Chambers was in May or June of 1936. He had said that time and again, but from the *Journal-American*'s account, you might not have been aware of this. The *Journal*'s opening paragraph that day read as follows, and we paraphrase a bit for all the clarity we can get: "Admitting he knew Chambers, Alger Hiss testified he last saw him in the spring of 1936—thus denying he lied to a grand jury in swearing he had not seen Chambers since January 1, 1937."

Now what in the world does that mean? All it does is haul in the word "lie" by the heels and twists the statement into emphasizing the point that Hiss knew Chambers at one time or another. The rest of the afternoon papers of that day played the story straight, with the *Sun* doing the best job. In fact, Harold Brown, representing the *Sun* at the trial, in our opinion merits commendation for having done the best all-around job of the afternoon paper reporters. In the morning field, the *Herald Tribune* and *Mirror* stories were consistently well balanced, and for the *News*, the team of James Desmond and Grace Robinson turned in well-written, well-balanced, and fair accounts. But on occasions, this very effort to keep in balance can lead to distortion, as it did in the *Times* of the next morning. The *Times* took so long getting around to the gist of Hiss's testimony that front-page readers were given more details of what Chambers had said about Hiss than of what Hiss had said in his own defense. William R. Conklin handled the story for the *Times*, and it began as follows: "Testifying for the second day in his own defense, Alger Hiss narrowed the issue of credibility between himself and Whittaker Chambers yesterday by entering denials of any spy-ring association with the former Communist underground leader." Permit us to enter a querulous parenthesis here: When, oh when, will newspaper reporters and editors throw into the wastebasket the tired old participial opening sentence—"testifying for the second day," "admitting that he knew . . ." Much simpler to begin simply with the statement that Alger Hiss testified for the second day, Alger Hiss admitted that he knew Whittaker Chambers.

But this is a lost cause—the participial opening line has been a fixture of journalism for so long that it is probably impossible to eradicate it, and we suppose the generations of young people advancing through schools of journalism will keep it by them always in their breathless effort to cram everything into the opening paragraph. But we like the comment of H. W. Fowler on the matter, to wit: "If newspaper editors, in the interest of their readers, maintain any discipline over the gentlemen who provide inch-long paragraphs to stop gaps, they should take measures against a particular form that, by a survival of the unfittest, bids fair to swallow up all others. In these paragraphs, before we are allowed to enter, we are challenged by the sentry, being a participle or some equivalent posted in advance to secure that our interview with . . . the subject of the sentence shall not take place without due ceremony."

Mr. Fowler is quite testy on the subject, and so are we, but we surrender and go back to the *New York Times*'s account of the second day of Alger Hiss's testimony. After that opening, which was fair, if participial, the story seemed to lean over backwards to balance Hiss's denials with the accusations made by Chambers a number of times before. After all, it was Hiss's day in court—he might well have been entitled to a showing for it. The *Times* story was filled with paragraphs like this—and we get another participle: "Still smiling and affable in the witness chair, the forty-four-year-old former State Department official gave a point-by-point refutation of the accusations made against him by Mr. Chambers. The government's chief witness (Chambers) had labeled Mr. Hiss and his wife Priscilla as Communist Party members and had testified that he received confidential State Department documents from Mr. Hiss manually in 1937 and 1938. . . . Mr. Chambers also told the jury . . . that his relationship with the Hisses began in May 1934 and extended on a basis of close friendship until April 1938."

This was followed by an eleven-line paragraph explaining that

Hiss had testified he had seen Chambers for the last time in June 1936 until he met him last year before the congressional committee. The story then went on, "Mr. Hiss contradicted the story of Mr. Chambers and his wife that she had first met them at the Chambers' home on Mount Royal Terrace in Baltimore in May 1934. From the beginning, Mr. Chambers had told the court that he obtained State Department documents through Mr. Hiss when the latter was legal counsel to the Senate Munitions Investigating Committee. The ex-Communist spy-ring courier also said that in January or February 1937, he had introduced Mr. Hiss to Col. Boris Bykov in the Prospect movie theater in Brooklyn." "Colonel Bykov," the *Times* went on, "was identified in a House committee report as a Soviet master spy in 1937 and 1938." The next paragraph of the *Times* story gave Chambers's version of what was described as the Hiss-Chambers-Bykov combination. At this point, there wasn't enough room to complete another *Times* paragraph on page 1, and the beginning of Hiss's refutation of the charges was begun on page 3. But what did remain on page 1 gives us a classic example of how a story can be colored, and alas, it gives us another initial participle.

It says, "Acknowledging that he knew Chambers under the name 'George Crosley,' Mr. Hiss painted quite a different picture yesterday. He portrayed himself on the stand as a Good Samaritan who had helped Crosley with small loans." Now the characterization of Hiss as a Good Samaritan was not the witness's own; it was the exclusive property of the *New York Times,* and its connection to Hiss's actual testimony seems somewhat remote.

To sum up, this *Times* story seemed to us to present Hiss's testimony in negative rather than positive form, but to balance this, it bought and printed the main portions of the transcript of Hiss's testimony as a supplement to its leading stories of the trial. We might also have a look at some headlines, which are extremely important in giving quick impressions to readers. The morning of June 28, for example—in the *Herald Tribune,* this way: "Hiss on stand four hours, holds to his story. Cross-examination leaves him calm. Clears up discrepancies on auto for Chambers and about typewriter." In the *Times*, it was this way: "Testimony of Hiss conflicts nine times, prosecutor finds. Cross-examination brings out 15 meetings with Chambers—10 or 11 were admitted. Clash on memorandums. Differences on typewriter and car transfer dates also noted by government." In the *News*, this way: "Gave Chambers a jalopy and brushoff, Hiss claims." In the *Mirror*: "Hiss says leftist friendship led to Red charges." You might not think it was practically the same story all these headlines were advertising.

Our best example of what you can do with actual testimony, though, comes on the afternoon of June 28. The *Journal-American*'s leading paragraph began as follows: "The government ended its cross-examination of Alger Hiss at 3:01 p.m. today after forcing him to admit he was an associate of Mrs. Carol King, prominent legal defender of Communists, and a friend of Nathan Witt, ex-New Deal lawyer who was fired because of his Communist activities." Now let's compare that with the transcript:

> QUESTION: Did you know Mrs. Carol King at the time?
>
> ANSWER: I think I met her once or twice during that period.
>
> QUESTION: So I think your answer is that you knew her?
>
> ANSWER: I said I think I met her once or twice; that is my answer.
>
> QUESTION: Was Nathan Witt one of the people in the association?
>
> ANSWER: I'm not sure whether he was or not. If so, that's how I met him. If not, I met him later while I was with the Department of Agriculture.

Now that question-and-answer transcript adds up to something rather different than what the *Journal-American* made of it in the opening paragraph of its story.

July 9, 1949

We'll return now to the matter which led to Judge Kaufman's comments about the press treatment of the trial—his comments which we'll repeat, in part: "This jury should not be influenced by outside sources. I have attempted to indicate to the jury that they have taken an oath at the commencement of this trial to try the case on the evidence as it is adduced in the courtroom without regard to what they see or hear outside. That is not evidence, and if we are going to get trials by publicity, the function of the courts will end." Judge Kaufman was referring to a story which was read in court by defense counsel Lloyd Paul Stryker; it had appeared in early editions of the *World-Telegram* of the day before, and it described an anti-Hiss pamphlet which had been written by William Marshall Bullitt, former solicitor general of the United States. The pamphlet said that John Foster Dulles, a trustee of the Carnegie Endowment for International Peace, had suggested that Hiss should resign as a trustee, although Hiss had testified to the contrary. The *Telegram*'s story ended with a question: "Who is lying—Mr. Dulles or Mr. Hiss?"

Stryker asked the court to consider a contempt action on the basis of this story, which the *Telegram*, incidentally, later denied that it had received from Mr. Bullitt in court. Judge Kaufman's comments then followed—also his references to columnists, some of whom had been at the trial, some of whom had not. The judge didn't name names, but Westbrook Pegler came out swinging: he had attended one session of the trial, part of another, and had used his visit to belabor Oliver Wendell Holmes, Felix Frankfurter, the New Deal, Henry L. Stimson, Dean Acheson, Prosecutor Murphy, Eleanor Roosevelt, and others too numerous to mention. Pegler read into the judge's comments a rap also at George Sokolsky of the *Sun*, and on June 30 he wrote, "Judge Kaufman is exercised over the uncomplimentary press he has been getting from George Sokolsky and me." "I name Mr. Sokolsky first only out of courtesy," Pegler continued, "because I believe his comments on the production under Judge Kaufman's supervision have been less opinionated than mine." The columnist went on to say that he deplores the trend and present state of affairs in the federal courts because the conditions have brought the integrity and honor of the national jurisprudence into question and disrepute with many citizens. And then there's a Peglerism which might stand as a model for many Pegler productions. He says, "I know nothing specifically about Judge Kaufman which I could allege as a contribution to this deplorable result." And that then serves as the point of departure for one of those sweeping Pegler denunciations which seem to take in so many people, from crooked labor leaders to the management of the *New York Herald Tribune.*

The sharpest comment on Pegler was contributed recently by Jimmy Wechsler, who has just taken over as editor of the *New York Post* and to whom our congratulations go. Jimmy wrote as follows:

> Not long ago Westbrook Pegler sadly confessed that innocent men and women have been hurt by reckless smears. Somebody must have promptly told Peg he was softening up; yesterday he was his robust self again. His *Journal-American* column contained a sentence which may appear in high-school textbooks as the classic example of guilt by association: "Although of course there is no charge of perjury against Mrs. Roosevelt in the Hiss case, she is co-defendant in a figurative sense because Hiss is a protégé of Felix Frankfurter, who has been a power behind the throne ever since the New Deal began."

And then Wechsler adds the snapper of his own: "And Westbrook Pegler is a Communist because he played poker with Heywood Broun, who was called a Communist by Martin Dies." And one final bit of Pegleriana which we submit without comment—he was referring to his forthcoming appearance before a congressional subcommittee to discuss labor unions, and on July 6 he advised his readers as follows: "The topic which this subcommittee has put to me is the absence of democracy in unions. I know little if anything about that because I am not interested in democracy anywhere except to oppose it. Where it isn't, I don't miss it." Pegler maintains this nation is a republic, but if you should take that statement at face value, he should enjoy life very much in Russia.

## August 20, 1949

Americans living with post-9/11 anxiety know firsthand the danger posed to the United States by its government and the news media regularly crying wolf about possible domestic terrorist threats. Does today's orange alert at the airport reflect the possibility of a real terrorist attack? Or is it merely a ploy to alarm the public and gain more support for the continued funding of American military actions in Iraq and Afghanistan? In the late 1940s and 1950s, the perceived threat of Communism caused the government and newspapers to cry wolf in ways that resonate today. In the midst of the Cold War, newspapers faced a temptation to hype stories that emphasized a scary Soviet threat, UN spies, an atomic bomb crisis, or other national-security disasters waiting to happen. In this broadcast, Hollenbeck described the flood of "scare-'em" reporting and explained its danger.

"BAD NEWS SELLS MORE newspapers than good news" might almost be a journalistic axiom, and some editors seem to operate on the theory that the human animal would rather have his flesh be made to creep by some account of dire happenings than read a less spine-tingling story which might conceivably tone down some of the sensational stuff. The possibility of war is always bad news, and we have recently been treated to some samples of how this theory of "scare-'em-and-make-'em-buy" operates. In the CBS newsroom early on the morning of July 26, a United Press bulletin came in. Under the signature of Edward V. Roberts, the bulletin read as follows: "The administration is preparing to lay before Congress secret intelligence reports which indicate that Russia is arming for war, it was learned today." The bulletin was amplified some time later by this: "Informed sources said American and allied agents have cracked the curtain of secrecy surrounding Soviet military preparations. Their reports, it was said, will be used to back up President Truman's request for a $1,450,000,000 arms aid program for free nations." The story then went on to say how many men it was thought Russia had under arms, how many operative war planes, how many naval craft, and so on. A pretty scary story on the basis of that first paragraph, although there was a sentence in the follow-up which made us thoughtful and made us wonder what the newspapers would do with the story.

That sentence we'll paraphrase: "The report will be used to back up President Truman's request for a $1,450,000,000 arms aid program." We were soon to find out how the press took to this story when the first editions of the afternoon papers came up. It wasn't in the early *Sun*, since that paper is not a United Press subscriber, but later editions carried a much less sensational AP version. It wasn't in the *World-Telegram*, which is a UP subscriber, and the omission seemed to be for a very special reason, which we'll discuss in a moment. It was in the *Post Home News* on page 4 under a big headline: "Red axis re-arming; six million in uniform." And it was very much in the *Journal-American*, which gave it the page-one red-ink banner line, "Report cites Red war plans." Next morning, the *Times* used the AP version in its first edition but dropped it later. The *Herald Tribune* mentioned the UP report near the end of its arms aid story, noting that the State Department declined to confirm it. The *News* and *Mirror* used the information in their running arms stories that morning. The *Compass* shied away from it. We'll go back to the *World-Telegram* now and possibly get at the reason the *World-Telegram* editors put the UP story on the dead-hook. For on the following day, the *World-Telegram* printed a story from Washington under the signature of Jim G. Lucas, and under the headline, "Will next U.S. war scare be wolf cry or real thing?" Lucas's story began as follows: "Are we due for a new war scare? If we are, how can we tell if it is real or phony?" He goes on to say that many high-ranking Washington leaders are skeptical of any imminent war but that many contradictions in policy statements have added to the confusion.

He points out that, two weeks earlier, John Foster Dulles had told the Senate that some unidentified members of the American delegation at Paris discussed the advisability of keeping the American people artificially alarmed—that they feared any relaxation of East-West tension would bring a corresponding relaxation on the part of the American people. Lucas then goes on to say that the disclosure that the administration was preparing to put before Congress secret intelligence reports on Russian military strength might possibly be a weapon to back up the military aid program. Now that had, of course, been explicitly stated in the United Press story of the day before but almost, as it were, in passing—as if it were simply an incidental to the main story.

And some other comments by Lucas helped to get things in better proportion. He pointed out that most of the figures used to support stories that Russia is arming for war have been known in Washington for some time—that military authorities say there has been no recent change for better or worse in Soviet-American relations. And, in conclusion, he makes a very significant observation: "The current crisis," he writes, "if one is developed, undoubtedly will be received with more skepticism than the last one." "At the same time," he says, "no one is inclined to dismiss it lightly. It might be a real wolf this time." Well, that's just it. There is always the possibility that there might be a wolf, and a reporter's and editor's job these days is to listen to the alarms with a critical ear and, in passing them along to readers, to point out plainly the possible reasons for them—as Hanson Baldwin in the *Times* did some days after that scare story when he wrote, "It is not necessary in order to justify the arms program to cry wolf prematurely, as some of the proponents of the plan have done in presenting it to Congress." "There is no present indication," Baldwin goes on, "of Russian intent to resort to armed force in the near future. . . . All indications are that there is no imminent danger of war." He points out that Russia's efforts at production of war material, the maintenance of the largest army in the world, her long-term preparations for war are well known. Also he points out that the United States and nearly every country in the world are making preparations for a war of the future.

A few days after this story on Russian military power and its varied treatment in the press, we had another which illustrated our thesis that the story which shocks or is spectacular is the story that most often commands the emphasis and the headlines. The sequel was provided by the Atomic Energy Commission's sixth semiannual report. Here are some of the headlines: In the *Daily News*: "A-superbomb output bared by AEC." The *Journal-American*: "Atom bomb in mass output." The *Herald Tribune*: "U.S. produces new deadlier atomic arms." Now from those headlines, one would not suspect that the bulk of the commission's report was devoted to an impressive and equally important list of peacetime atomic-energy advances. *Time* magazine devoted most of its story to the peacetime aspects of the report and pointed out, "The report says little about A-bombs. Its six vague pages entitled 'military application' sound like a Soviet report on the current five-year plan. 'New and more atomic weapons' which were tested at Eniwetok in 1948 are in production. That is about all." "There is not a firm figure," *Time* goes on, "to inform, alarm, or comfort the nation's potential foes or friends." As for the metropolitan press, its handling of this phase of the report is interesting. The *Post* was the only daily which emphasized the peacetime phases; Charles Van Devander's story from Washington pointed out that the military aspects were touched on only lightly, and he dealt at length with the progress achieved in the field of doing some good for mankind rather than knocking its brains out. The *Telegram* had an adequate story on peacetime progress, but the page-one headline was on the bomb.

The *Compass* story we saw didn't even mention nonmilitary progress; in the *News* and *Mirror*, it got one brief paragraph. In the *Herald Tribune* story, it was said that the report was studded with hitherto unrevealed material on atomic radiation, medicine, and biology—fields which a top scientist described as virtually a second world for study and exploration. That would seem to be pretty important—worth considerably more attention than it got in the press generally. But without doubt, the word "bomb" is more attention-compelling than the word "isotope" and is more likely to persuade one to buy a newspaper.

We have still one more item in our "scare-'em" exhibit, and for that one, we'll go back a little in time. In July 1948 testimony before a Senate judiciary subcommittee was made public, and it brought a rash of alarming headlines such as this one: "UN a clock for Red spies, Congress told." In the *New York Times*: "Subversive agents believed in U.S. under wing of UN. Officials of State Department say several hundred are here and protected by pacts." Just seven days after that story made headlines, the then secretary of state George Marshall appointed a committee to investigate the charges which had been made before the Senate group by three minor State Department officials. One member of Marshall's committee was a newspaperman, Benjamin McKelway, editor of the *Washington Star*. After one month's investigation, the committee reported back—reported it was shocked at the manner in which irresponsible charges were made against the United Nations.

The committee said it did find a calculated risk and a degree of potential danger to our national security in admitting into the United States aliens who are antagonistic to our form of government, but it added that the UN is one of the great hopes for that very security. It found that regulations covering the admission of UN-connected aliens were adequate to safeguard the security of the United States, and they were properly applied. Commenting on the matter editorially, the *New York Times* said, "The charges were made public by the congressional committee and naturally received wide attention in American newspapers. Rarely have such accusations been answered as speedily and completely as these have now been."

"The tragedy of the matter is," the *Times* said, "that such disavowals as those made by responsible State Department officials of these slanderous attacks on United Nations personnel . . . never completely catch up with the charges." "Even if they could," the *Times* went on, "it is doubtful that the rebuttals would completely cleanse the minds of the distrust placed by the original statements." But that was by no means the end of it. Seven months later we got it all again. On April 26 a brief Associated Press dispatch in the *Times* quoted Senator Pat McCarran of Nevada as saying that the subcommittee had conclusive and alarming evidence of extensive subversive activity being carried on in this country, under the direction of foreign agents. The reason for the senator's remarks was that he had introduced legislation to strengthen immigration laws and tighten defenses against espionage. But the big blow-off came last month—July 23—when the Senate committee which was taking testimony in connection with Senator McCarran's legislation released a humdinger for the following day's papers. The committee made public testimony of "witness number eight," not otherwise identified. The mystery witness charged that Communist pressure on UN employees comes from the top; that UN officials from democratic countries fail to resist it; and that Reds seek to use the secretariat and UN services for Soviet purposes. This witness, the committee said, proposed that the senators seek the ouster of Mr. Lie and urged that a "capable" successor be appointed. In New York, acting UN secretary general Byron Price called the testimony fantastically untrue and said the story was "the nuttiest story I have heard yet."

Most of the papers used the Washington story sparingly, but the *Mirror* and the *Journal-American* jumped on it. In an eight-column, double-banner headline, the *Journal*'s first edition said, "Lie 'terrorizes' UN to force Reds on staff, senators told." The lead on its story went this way: "Trygve Lie, secretary general of the United

Nations, was accused in congressional testimony released today of 'terrorizing' his staff into loading the UN with Communists and fellow travelers." The *Mirror* that morning carried a big front-page headline, too. "Charges Red aides dominate UN," it said. The headline on its story on page 2: "Lie packs UN with Reds by 'terror' methods." The *Times,* apparently wary of the story, put it back on page 10. The *Tribune* and the *News* gave it better play. The next day—Monday—an eighteen-member staff committee of the UN secretariat voted full support of Mr. Lie and denounced the charges as unsubstantiated and reprehensible.

Then on August 1, the *Journal-American* got out the red ink for its headline over an exclusive International News Service story from Washington. "Bare Red spy underground," said the big, red, eight-column, front-page headline. "Senator McCarran," the story began, "today declared an 'underground railroad' brings thousands of Communist spies and propagandists into the United States each year." The senator was reported as asserting they cross the Canadian and Mexican borders virtually unchecked, and he said that others come in with "immunity visas" as employees of the UN or other international organizations. Well, nobody else had this story for awhile. UP finally got it from the senator, and the *World-Telegram* used it in late editions of that day. AP didn't bother with it until later that evening, when the *Compass* asked for it, because, one AP editor said, it didn't seem like anything new to him. Anyway, AP called Senator McCarran and got the story, too. The *News* didn't bother with it; neither did the *Post* or the *Sun.* The *Times* carried about three and a half inches on page 9, the *Tribune* about the same space on page 6. Next day the *Journal-American* had the field to itself and another big red headline: "Trace spy smuggling to UN," it said. It was an INS story that began this way: "An 'underground railroad' bringing in foreign agents is reported today to be linked 'directly to at least one United Nations delegate' from a Russian-dominated country."

The story said the source declined to be identified but that it was close to the Senate subcommittee investigating subversive aliens in the United States. We couldn't find that story any other place that day or the next morning—August 3—with the exception of the *Mirror*. On the third, the *Mirror*, which hadn't carried the first INS story, brought its readers up to date with a round-up of the changes made during the past two days.

The following day—August 4—the *Times* and the *Tribune* carried full-column stories reporting the contents of a letter Secretary of State Dean Acheson had written to Byron Price indicating he placed no credence in the secret testimony released to the press alleging "red terror" in the United Nations. The secretary of state said, the papers reported, that he was confident that a situation like this described by the anonymous witness would not be tolerated.

There are three exhibits of the "scare-'em" school: frightening Russian war plans, our atom bomb in mass output, the flood of subversive agents into this country. There might be something to that story as reported by Jim Lucas—that some policy makers believe in keeping the American people artificially alarmed just so we won't relax. If that's going to be the policy, we wish the press would remind us of it more often—it's hard to get any work done.

## September 3, 1949

Hollenbeck's broadcast this day focused on newspapers' role in perhaps the most dramatic physical confrontation of the domestic Cold War. Paul Robeson, a legendary black athlete, lawyer, actor, civil rights activist, and singer, had been honored in the 1940s by labor unions with life memberships and requests to perform at their national conventions and march in their picket lines. By 1949, however, the pressure on labor unions to contain Communism and expel radicals made Robeson's militancy unacceptable. His U.S. concerts were canceled. He toured Europe, criticized U.S. government racism, and supported the Soviet Union, where people had welcomed him warmly beginning with his first visit in 1934. The announcement that Robeson would give a benefit concert near Peekskill for the Harlem chapter of the Civil Rights Congress, labeled subversive by former attorney general Tom Clark, outraged local veterans' groups. Rioting broke up the scheduled concert and led to press coverage that suggested, Hollenbeck said, that objectivity appeared to be "going out of fashion."

IN CONSIDERING THE PRESS's treatment of last Saturday night's big story—the rioting at Peekskill, in which nine people were hurt and which broke up a scheduled concert by Paul Robeson—we must widen our sights and include in the discussion the out-of-town press. We must also consider the power of publicity, and in the case of the Peekskill trouble, it was to a very great extent the power of publicity which began the series of events which were climaxed last Saturday night. In New York City we are sometimes inclined to overlook the very real power of the press; in fact, in New York and other great cities, the press by no means possesses the influence it does in smaller communities. The big papers may exhort, bemoan, praise, or belabor; they may or may not get something accomplished. But when a smaller journal in a more closely knit community goes after something, things are bound to happen. What happened at Peekskill Saturday night may be traced pretty directly to the power of publicity and the influence of a community newspaper. Five days before Robeson's scheduled concert, the *Peekskill Evening Star* published a front-page story about it, pointing out that the concert was to be sponsored by People's Artists Inc., an organization tagged as subversive by the California Committee on Un-American Activities, and said the concert was in aid of the Harlem chapter of the Civil Rights Congress, which has also been labeled subversive by the former attorney general Tom Clark.

The story went into detail about Robeson's pro-Communist sympathies and activities, and in that same issue of Tuesday, August 23, there was an editorial and a letter to the editor. The editorial deplored Robeson's political opinions and said that every ticket purchased for the concert would drop nickels and dimes into the till basket of an un-American political organization. It concluded with these words: "The time for tolerant silence that signifies approval is running out. Peekskill wants no rallies that support iron curtains, concentration camps, blockades, and NKVDs, no matter how masterful the decor, nor how sweet the music." The letter to the editor was signed by Vincent Boyle, and one paragraph in it pointed out that, some years ago, the Ku Klux Klan appeared in the nearby community of Verplanck and received their just reward. The writer referred to a beating that had been given the Kluxers by the local residents, after which they let the community strictly alone. And his letter went on, "I am not intimating violence in this case, but I believe we should give this matter serious consideration and strive to find a remedy that will cope with the situation the same way as Verplanck and with the same result—that they will never reappear in this area. . . . If we have not forgotten the war, then let us cooperate with the American Legion and similar veteran organizations and vehemently oppose their appearance or reappearance." In this case, it was obviously not the Kluxers to whom the letter writer was referring—it was Paul Robeson and those of his political persuasion. Next day, the *Star* carried on; it reported criticism of the concert by the Peekskill Chamber of Commerce but said that legally, the concert could not be halted.

The town of Cortlandt, within whose limits it was scheduled, does not require the issuance of a permit for a public gathering, the paper said, and if the audience at such a meeting conducts itself in a peaceful manner and does not cause a disturbance, the meeting could not be prevented. At the same time, the *Star* announced that a meeting of veterans' organizations had been called and that Victor Sharrow, a labor party official, had appealed to Attorney General Nathaniel Goldstein in Albany. The paper quoted Sharrow's telegram to Goldstein as saying that the *Star* had published an article and an editorial which Sharrow contended advocated citizens "to do something to see to it that this affair is disrupted or to see that it is not carried out in a peaceful manner." Parenthetically, the *Star* commented that it had merely revealed the nature of the organizations sponsoring the concert and that they would benefit by the ticket sales. On Thursday, the *Star* reported that angry veterans had made plans to stage a protest parade near the concert scene and also that there had been other requests to state and county officials pointing out the possibility of violence. By Friday, the *Star* was trying to calm things down a little; in a front-page editorial it said, "At no time, either in its news columns or editorially, has the *Evening Star* ever advocated 'violence' as a means of disrupting this or any other kind of program. We did state, however, and do here reaffirm, our conviction that the time for tolerant silence that signifies approval has run out, and that it is high time to speak forth."

The *Star* commended the veterans' groups on their plans for a peaceful protest, and it urged citizens of the community to do their part by staying away from the concert. In the same issue, the *Star* printed letters to the editor in support of the concert, one of them from Victor Sharrow of the labor party asking that the *Star*, since it had created so much publicity about the concert, state unequivocally its opposition to any form of organized or unorganized action that would create or tend to create an incident of any kind. An editor's note appended to the letter pointed out that the *Star*'s page-one editorial of that date covered this point.

Donald Ikeler, general manager of the *Star*, amplified this for CBS. He said that in using the phrase, "The time for tolerant silence that signifies approval is running out," the newspaper had intended only to suggest that people speak out against the concert—that peaceful picketing or a boycott of it would be effective. Saturday's *Star* estimated that upwards of five thousand people would jam the line of march for the protest, that probably not more than two thousand would attend the concert itself, that there would be no extra details of state police on hand. It also quoted the opinion of a Peekskill attorney that so long as ticket holders were not prevented from entering the concert grounds, the protest meeting was entirely legal. But the momentum had been gained; the words "violence," "anger," "disturbance," and so on had been used so often that the stage had been set for the trouble which resulted. And after it was over, the *Peekskill Evening Star* printed an editorial that outdid some of those in our own New York papers. It said, "Regardless of the extent of provocation to violence, of which there can be no accurate calculation by either side at this time, the fact remains that disrespect of law and order has no valid excuse. And the constitutional right of free assembly which was infringed on Saturday night is a fact which also must be regretted by all citizens."

This is a far cry from the *Star*'s editorial of a week before—the one which said, "The time for tolerant silence that signifies approval is running out. Peekskill wants no rallies that support iron curtains, concentration camps, blockades, and NKVDs, no matter how masterful the decor nor how sweet the music."

Now to the treatment of the story by the New York metropolitan press. Peekskill correspondents of the big newspapers handled the job, and in a riotous situation, they did an extremely good job, so far as reporting as well as they could what went on. There were some of the usual conflicting figures, but on the whole, a satisfactory job was turned in. The United Press was ahead of almost everybody with its account, furnished to them by the news staff of station WLNA, including news editor Ray LaPolla, Francis Lough, and two other staff members who were on the scene from the beginning; Lapolla recruited four other volunteers to help in the coverage of what one WLNA news broadcast called one of the biggest stories ever to develop in the Peekskill area. By Monday, the New York newspapers had begun to print editorials on the affair, and some of them provided food for thought—the *Mirror,* for instance, which said, "War veterans demonstrating against Robeson clashed with his supporters Saturday. That is too bad. Riots are ugly things. But Robeson has been asking for it." The *News* took pretty much the same point of view when it said, "Most Americans, especially young veterans who recently fought to save their country, are not much impressed by fine legal distinctions. Their tendency is to go in for some direct and hard-boiled action when they run afoul of people whom they know to be bent on overturning our government and making slaves of us all." "Again," the *News* says, "these riots are deplorable. But as long as the domestic Reds and their cronies have this double standing before the law, we think these riots are going to occur from time to time."

Very much in contrast to these points of view is that taken by the *New York Times,* which pulled no punches Monday morning. It asked what Paul Robeson's political ideas, however misguided, have to do with his right to sing. "Or," said the *Times,* "if a man can be enjoined from singing in public in this free country because his opinions are wrong and illogical shall the injunction be enforced by mob action?" "We think," the *Times* said, "these questions answer themselves. Lamenting the twisted thinking that is ruining Paul Robeson's great career, we defend his right to carry his art to whatever peaceably assembled groups of people he wishes. That is the American way."

Some of the other editorial comment was less forthright than this of the *Times*—or of the *News* and *Mirror*, which almost seemed to condone the violence. The *Sun* found that it was perhaps not altogether surprising that emotions boiled over at Peekskill, although it deplored the rioting and pointed out that it had simply provided the Communists with an opportunity to pose as martyrs and to intensify their diatribes against America, citing the rioting as an example of an American attitude which proclaims liberty for all but makes distinctions in granting it. This point of view was also expressed by the *Herald Tribune*, although it said that whether there was any provocation to violence beyond the concert itself is not known. *Time* magazine described the affair as an example of misguided patriotism and senseless hooliganism more useful to Communist propaganda than a dozen uninterrupted song recitals by Paul Robeson. The *Post Home News* and the *Compass* were the most indignant over the incident. The *Post* professed to see the Ku Klux Klan in the background, and there were a number of stories about a cross having been burned, although it hasn't been possible to confirm this. Editor Ted Thackrey of the *Compass* wrote Tuesday's story himself and began it as follows: "The budding storm troopers of Peekskill and surrounding Westchester County, under the benevolent protection of county and state officers, staged a Munich-style putsch at Lakeland Acres Saturday night, complete with such native American-Fascist touches as blazing Ku Klux Klan crosses."

Accompanying this inflammatory story is a gruesome picture of an unidentified woman with a black eye, described in the caption as having suffered the injury at the hands of hoodlums at the concert. Perhaps the most frightening pictorial job was done by the *Daily News*. Monday morning's page 1 was given over to a very uncomplimentary photograph of Paul Robeson at a news conference by Walter Kelleher, a photograph which portrayed

Robeson as anything but one of the greatest singers of our time—it made him rather an ogre. The *News*, though, seemed to think so highly of it that it reprinted it next day in smaller size as an illustration in that editorial, which looked with understanding on the tendency of Americans to go in for some direct and hard-boiled action when they run afoul of people whom—that's the word the *News* used—whom they know to be bent on overturning our government and making slaves of us all.

In the follow-up stories, there were some interesting points, too. The *World-Telegram* quoted Donald Ikeler of the *Peekskill Star* as saying that there would have been no rioting if it hadn't been for the stabbing of one of the veterans, but that doesn't square with what reporters on the scene say, nor did Ikeler's own paper tell that story in its account of the rioting. A number of reporters interviewed by CBS agreed that sometime before the stabbing, there had been a number of violent encounters.

You can report a story of this sort from any point of view you like—that's pretty well illustrated in two contrasting cases: the *World-Telegram* and the *Compass.* The *Telegram* has concentrated on getting its stories from anti-Robeson sources. The *Compass* has gone to the other extreme, even to the point of helping to maintain a scare atmosphere, reporting that residents of the neighborhood are closing up their homes and leaving because they are afraid of what might happen to them. The observation has been made that reporting of stories of this sort tend to subjectivity—that the reporter's own emotions and opinions become involved, or rather, in many cases, the emotions and opinions of his newspaper become involved, and he gets the story he is sent to get. In a story involving as much political tinder as the Paul Robeson concert story did—even before it began, as we've seen by studying the case of the *Peekskill Star*—objectivity seems almost impossible. But, alas, objectivity rather seems to be going out of fashion these days, so perhaps it's only a sign of the times.

## September 10, 1949

The symbiotic relationship between William Laurence, a *New York Times* science reporter, and the government during World War II raised a question also asked during the Iraq War about the embedded reporter: Does a journalist have to cooperate with the government to obtain full access to the facts? Laurence repeatedly submitted articles about atomic energy, weapons, and uranium to the government's office of press censorship. The stories were "returned with the request not to publish."[1] In 1945 Gen. Leslie R. Groves of the Manhattan Project asked the *Times* to allow Laurence to work with him as "the official historian of the atomic-bomb project."[2] To keep Laurence's role secret, the *Times* lied in print about his whereabouts. Laurence, who drafted government press releases about atomic-bomb tests and wrote what became the basis of President Truman's half-hour radio address following the atomic attack on Hiroshima, was proud of his "service to the nation."[3] General Groves and the government also were of service to Laurence. He was the only journalist permitted to witness—from the safety of a U.S. plane—the atomic bombing of Nagasaki. His wartime coverage won a Pulitzer Prize in 1946.

OCCASIONALLY, A NEWSPAPERMAN is called upon to be more than a newspaperman, more than simply a reporter of events. He may take a hand now and then in the shaping of those events, and quite often he must play detective. It is as a detective plus diplomat and humanitarian that we today consider William L. Laurence, reporter-extraordinary for the *New York Times*, and as a very special sort of detective, too. No gumshoe work trying to

1. William L. Laurence, *Men and Atoms: The Discovery, the Use and the Future of Atomic Energy* (New York: Simon and Schuster, 1959), 95.
2. Laurence, *Men and Atoms*, 96.
3. Laurence, *Men and Atoms*, 113.

solve a murder mystery, no digging into musty police records to come up with shocking revelations—none of the customary kind of detective work which good police reporters know how to do so well. Laurence's detective work was in his own special department of science, and as our story unfolds, it will become apparent that he is without question head and shoulders above anybody else in that field. And that field is a big one; as he once told his Harvard classmates in an anniversary report, "I have been covering news in the realm of science, from astronomy to zoology and intermediate points. The infinitesimal and the infinite, from metagalaxies to microbes, constitute my present domain. I report news about the Einstein relativity and unified field theories, quantum mechanics, the cosmic ray, and the nucleus of the atom. I annihilate the universe with Eddington and put it together again with Millikan. If you want to know about genes and chromosomes, enzymes, hormones, vitamins, electrons, protons, neutrons, and morons, read the *New York Times*."

But in the *Times* itself, there was very little of this fascinating detective and diplomatic story. We came across it in a *Times* house publication, and we retell it here so that more people than *Times* employees can know that Bill Laurence wasn't overstating it when he outlined his range of reporting for his Harvard classmates. But first, a quick biographical portrait: William Leonard Laurence is a short, fair man, getting on for sixty-one. He was born in Lithuania, and his family name was Siew Zeeve. He came to America in 1905 and did odd jobs, including baby-sitting, until he finished high school in Roxbury, Massachusetts, where he was so impressed with the place that he took as his last name the name of the Roxbury street where he lived—it was, he says, his first real home. Bill Laurence has been a science reporter for the *Times* for nearly twenty years, and during those years, he has made some notable achievements. That he was the first scientific reporter to understand and explain the story of atomic energy is well known—his understanding and his reporting were so expert that he was called in by the government to help prepare the statements which explained to the public just what was going on. This latest exploit caused Arthur Krock of the *Times* Washington office to tell Laurence that whatever other triumphs he may have, Krock doubted that any would surpass this. So without more ado, we'll get to the story of that triumph.

On August 16, a story on page 1 of the *Times* under Laurence's signature began as follows: "The seed of an African plant holds the answer to the prayers of millions for cortisone, the recently synthesized adrenal gland hormone that pours buoyant new life into bodies tortured by arthritis and rheumatic fever, and promises new hope for victims of other chronic ills, as well as the mentally afflicted." It was one of the most interesting and important science stories we've ever read—details of how this plant had been searched for, how it was discovered, and how now, as Laurence wrote, it is expected to become one of the most important plants in the world, serving as the source of a veritable elixir of life to millions of persons the world over. But not one word of that story told how important a part Bill Laurence himself had played in the plant's discovery, and that's our job here.

Last April Laurence went to a demonstration at the Mayo Clinic in Rochester, Minnesota. There he saw a medical miracle: fourteen men and women hopelessly crippled by arthritis left their beds and wheelchairs to walk briskly after injections of a synthetic drug called cortisone. But that cortisone could be obtained only in minute quantities; its base is ox bile, and a single-day's treatment for one patient required bile from forty head of cattle. To produce a three-week supply for one patient cost $18,000. Also, it must be given continuously since it is not a cure, and once it is stopped, the relief is gone.

Laurence had an exclusive story on that miracle, but he didn't let it go at that—he started his job of detective work. He asked a scientist if it might not be possible to find some comparatively cheap substitute for this costly ox bile. The scientist remembered that a certain plant seed yielded a cortisone base, but he was vague, so Laurence asked more questions of chemists. One told him that the name of the substance yielded by the plant seed was sarmentogenin but that it wasn't known what plant it came from, and Laurence was referred to Dr. Walter Jacobs of the Rockefeller Institute. Dr. Jacobs told him that thirty-four years ago, the institute had received a shipment of mislabeled seed; instead of yielding a compound they were looking for, it yielded sarmentogenin. But none of that seed was saved, and even later, when the institute researchers got more of the compound, they did nothing about it—there was no call for cortisone then. Now, as the *Times* story says, Bill Laurence became a feverishly medical Sherlock Holmes.

He plunged deeply into German medical lore in the public library, and he learned from this research that there was just one plant—the flowering sarmentosus—which held the elusive seed. From the Bronx Botanical Gardens he got pictures of this plant, and then he got his first real hot clue: somebody told him that a group of Swiss researchers had got on the trail and were sending an expedition to Africa to gather a crop of the seeds. Incidentally, Bill Laurence had done all this investigating on his own time; nobody at the *Times* office had any idea of what he was up to. By the time he had learned what the plant was, he figured he ought to write a story about it, and he started to do so. But here is where Bill Laurence switched from being a detective and became a diplomat. He realized that the story had enormous political and economic implications. He figured that if the plant were available only in British-controlled Africa, its discovery might cause the British to put an embargo on its export in order to maintain a monopoly, and he realized that here was a story which had to be told first to the president of the United States.

Laurence put through a call to the White House, and a conference was arranged. He asked the city desk for a day off and went down to Washington; he was still doing all this on his own. At that conference with President Truman, he made it plain that this discovery is to medicine what atomic energy is to physics, and he had no difficulty in convincing the president of its importance. He suggested that experts be sent at once to equatorial Africa to gather a supply of seeds and living plants. He said he knew that, at present, only the Swiss were aware of their importance and might even be taking steps to bottle up the entire supply. Secretary of Agriculture [Charles] Brannan and Federal Security Administrator [Oscar] Ewing were consulted, and Laurence emphasized the need for haste. The plant blooms in early fall, and young seeds contain most of the material. If it weren't found by September, there would be a year's lag.

Bill Laurence returned to New York, this time without a story; it had been agreed that for obvious reasons, nothing could be made public. A few days later, Laurence got a call from Dr. Leonard Scheele, surgeon general of the public health service. "An expedition has just left for Africa," Dr. Scheele told Laurence. "It's headed for Liberia—the plant grows there, too." A reporter never got a better break than that. There was no longer any reason for secrecy since large sums of American capital have been invested in developing Liberian resources, and there could be no more valuable raw material for medicine than the seeds of the flowering sarmentosus, which Bill Laurence had been hunting since April. But the story wasn't published just yet. There was another Washington conference at which it was agreed that Laurence was to have the story exclusively, but the surgeon general said somewhat pathetically, "Please leave us something to announce," and Laurence generously agreed to omit from his first account the fact that an expedition was already on its way to Liberia. Laurence's story appeared on August 16, and next day another *Times* story by Bess Furman told how the expedition was on its way. That story, in a very modest way, gave Laurence credit for getting things started, but until now, a detailed account of his detective-diplomatic achievement hasn't been told, and it is a real pleasure to repeat the words of Arthur Krock to Bill Laurence: "The press conference today based on your cortisone discovery officially recognized a great feat of journalism and humanitarianism. Whatever other triumphs you may have, I doubt that any will surpass this."

Now that the epidemic of English Channel swimming seems to be over—for the season, at least—and Shirley May France is headed back to school at Somerset, Massachusetts, we can consider some of the journalistic aspects of the phenomenon. And we can begin with a pretty safe generalization, contributed by David Schoenbrun of our Paris bureau. "The correspondents," he cabled us, "are so sick of channel swimmers that they can't even look at filet of sole without shuddering." There were about twenty of these crossing attempts, of which two were successful, but of course, the Shirley May expedition commanded the most attention from the press. We got dispatches with such datelines as "Aboard the *Black Magic*," "Aboard the *Red Commodore* in the English Channel," and "Airborne over the English Channel." That dispatch, by the Associated Press, informed us that from the air, the Shirley May flotilla looked like a children's game of ring-around-a-rosy, with the press boats and all. A pretty figure, but to the correspondents assigned, it was a less-jolly game. Let a veteran reporter who also reports the French cabinet and parliament outline some of the problems. "It's like being a war correspondent again without a war," he says.

> Calais is a beat-up channel port, covered with rubble. It's about fifteen miles from Cap Gris Nez, where the swimmers take off, and it's the only town large enough to carry a wire-photo line to Paris. We rented a room in a garage in Wissant, a village three miles from the beach. The proprietor of the garage hates everybody in the world, particularly swimmers and reporters. Here's a sample—our photographer asked him if he had a telephone. "Why?" asked the proprietor.

"To make a telephone call," the photographer came back. "To where?" was the proprietor's reaction to this. "To Paris," was the weary explanation. "We haven't got a telephone," the proprietor said, and that took care of that.

And the swimmers weren't the only ones who faced perils. The night the Cuban swimmer Cortinas took off, that same photographer waded out deep and set off a magnesium flare, which the wind whipped back on him, burning up his coat and pants. He lost his shoes in the surf, worked barefoot all night, then drove a jeep fifteen miles to the darkroom in Calais. When Shirley May got to town, she hid from the reporters, so they had to play detective for five hours and then discovered her promoters had made special commitments under which her interviews and photographs were restricted to certain organizations. Editors in Paris who handled the story from there said that the wordage on the channel circuses almost equaled that devoted to the opening sessions of the Council of Europe at Strasbourg. And so on. It all seems scarcely worth it, but such things are operated on the theory that reporters and photographers get what people are really interested in, and perhaps the public interest in these attempts to knock yourself out swimming thirty miles or so really warrant the attention they get: for the Shirley May flotilla, as the Associated Press called it, a schooner, a diesel ship, a pilot boat, row boats and speed boats, and the international press corps—a hundred reporters—with their walkie-talkie telephones, powerful cameras, rocket signals, carrier pigeons, and an astronomical telescope through which to . . . usually gawk at the planet Jupiter.

Consider the case of Robert Musel of the United Press, one of the best reporters in the business: on the Shirley May swim, he was jumping from speedboat to pilot boat, drenched with rain and spray, forced to bail continuously. And finally, when it was all over, Bob walked into Shirley May's hotel room in Dover for a final interview—his soggy felt hat shapeless and dripping, his clothes soaked, his face unshaven, and his eyes bleary after twenty-four sleepless hours. Shirley May was crying over her failure, but as she looked up at Bob she said, "Gosh, it looks like you had a worse time than I did." And Musel agreed that she was right.

Just listen to the ordeal of a couple of reporters: Musel and Dan Gilmore lost their way in their small boat when Shirley May's swim began—had to bail continuously to keep afloat. Their portable walkie-talkie set got wet and sometimes wouldn't work, so they had to holler much of their information, jumping from pilot boat to press boat and back again, trying to be heard above the phonograph records which were being played to hearten Shirley May on her swim. Finally, the walkie-talkie set went completely out of commission, but Gilmore, an air-force veteran, repaired it with a can opener and a bobby pin which he had borrowed from a woman passenger. You get some real adventure in the English Channel.

Somehow no story of channel swimming will ever appeal to us quite as much as the story told by Al Laney in his book *Paris Herald, the Incredible Newspaper*. In 1925 the swimmers had gathered, and the reporters had gathered with them, although the collection and dissemination of news was much simpler then—no walkie-talkie telephones, no rocket signals, no wirephoto lines to Paris. The reporters were just as bored then as they are now with the job of trailing grease-smeared swimmers around, and two of them were so fed up that, between them, they concocted the best story ever to come out of a channel swim, even if it was a hoax. The real swimmers made dull copy, so to confuse a colleague and provide some excitement, Tom Topping of the Associated Press and Fred Abbott of International News Service invented a channel swimmer that we wish had been a real one: he was Itchy Guk, an Eskimo who lived in the icebox at Harry's New York Bar in Paris. But the really fascinating thing about Itchy Guk was that he couldn't swim the English Channel because the water was too warm. We wish he had been present to furnish some comic relief in the current extravaganza.

## November 12, 1949

Hollenbeck began this broadcast about his foot-rule survey of news coverage of candidates for mayor of New York by letting Mayor William O'Dwyer speak for himself. Hollenbeck's *CBS Views the Press* allowed listeners, in a way then unavailable to newspaper and magazine readers, to be present at events—to hear an angry O'Dwyer, to experience a honking *Mirror* photographer's radio car racing a siren-screaming ambulance to an accident scene, to listen to the disconsolate employees of the *Star* and *Sun* as they published for the last time. The broadcasts were more powerful and persuasive because they were heard, not read. Marshall McLuhan explained, "Radio affects most people intimately, person-to-person, offering a world of unspoken communication between writer-speaker and the listener."[1] The pauses, the silences between words, the sound effects, the background sounds—all communicated in important ways to Hollenbeck's audience.[2]

WE'LL OPEN UP TONIGHT by letting another voice—a recorded one—set our text, and here it is:

**Tape Cue #1**

I am happy at this moment in one great respect. Despite the fact that a campaign of filth and dirt, unmatched in this city in all its history, [was run] by the opposition to us; despite the fact that they were supported wholeheartedly by practically all the newspapers; nevertheless, neither the bilge, the filth, nor the newspapers were able to fool or

1. Marshall McLuhan, *Understanding Media: The Extensions of Man* (New York: McGraw-Hill Book Company, 1965), 299.
2. On Hollenbeck's use of sound effects to create mood, see Graud Chester and Garnet R. Garrison, *Radio and Television: An Introduction* (New York: Appleton-Century-Crofts, 1950), 421–22.

> change the minds of the people. The people are not as easily fooled as the newspapers and the politicians that opposed us thought they were going to be.

That is an angry man speaking; that is Mayor William O'Dwyer making some remarks on the radio on election night that we didn't see widely printed in the newspapers, and the remarks might well be supplemented by another quotation. This one is from a book called *Your Newspaper*, written by a group of newspapermen during their Nieman Fellowship year at Harvard University. They wrote,

> The American popular press reached a peak of public leadership, for better or worse, at the turn of the century. . . . It was a period when the press gained great prestige by exposure of political corruption.
>
> Led by vigorous newspapers that took an active part in trust-busting campaigns and championing Woodrow Wilson's idealistic conception of democracy, the press maintained its great influence through the First World War. Today the newspapers, while still powerful, have lost their leadership. Readers no longer look to them for advice and wisdom in making great decisions.

Now with those two quotations in mind, let us examine the performance of the New York metropolitan press during part of the political campaign just concluded. In the first place, only one of the major newspapers supported Mayor O'Dwyer: that was the *Daily Mirror*, which made up its mind at the last minute and can't be said to have conducted a very sustained campaign for the mayor's reelection. The mayor also had the support of the *Brooklyn Eagle*, *Il Progresso*, the Italian-language newspaper, the *Jewish Day*, and the *Long Island Star-Journal*. That's all—the rest of the papers, with a combined weekday circulation of nearly five million a day, were against him or did not actively support him, which amounts to about the same thing so far as a political candidate is concerned. Most of the press, too, was against former governor Herbert H. Lehman in his campaign against John Foster Dulles for the United States Senate. As everyone knows now, O'Dwyer and Lehman came out on top, in the face of opposition or silence on the part of the big majority of the city's newspapers. On a local scale, it seemed to have been last November all over again—another occasion when the people snubbed the press at the polling places. But there was a sign or two that perhaps a lesson had been learned last autumn, in the case of the *Journal-American*, for instance.

The *Journal* is the city's most widely circulated evening newspaper—it has more than seven hundred thousand daily readers and is a publication of great influence. Yet in this election, the *Journal* plugged for no candidates at all; in an editorial just before election day, it seemed to call a plague on all the candidates' houses, and yet in capital letters, it exhorted the citizenry to exercise its right to VOTE. The *Journal* apparently was taking no chances on miscalling its shots. Although the *Journal* itself took no editorial stand on the candidates, its number-one columnist did: Westbrook Pegler denounced both O'Dwyer and Newbold Morris as inferior men and advanced a candidate of his own, Robert Moses, who wasn't running but who didn't like Franklin D. Roosevelt, which is good enough for Pegler.

The *New York Times* and the *Herald Tribune* came out flatly for Newbold Morris and John Foster Dulles; the *Daily News* straddled the question of the mayor and, with some reservations, liked Dulles better than Lehman. On the day before the election, the *Mirror* made its favorite team O'Dwyer and Dulles, it was unstinting in its praise of O'Dwyer's record in office, and, along with the mayor, the *Mirror* recommended the election of his teammates Comptroller Lazarus Joseph and Council President Vincent Impelliterri. The *World-Telegram* liked Morris and Dulles, and it predicted a close election, which it wasn't; one *Telegram* headline said, "Senate race a toss-up," and in the same issue a Gallup poll showed Lehman to be leading by 12 percent. The *Sun* came out for Dulles, but in the mayoralty campaign, it made no definite recommendation; indeed, it chided Morris for making political capital out of the presence of O'Dwyer at a Democratic Party dinner also attended by Lehman and by the gambler Frank Erickson. The *Sun* said if Morris was trying to get votes by denouncing O'Dwyer for attending that dinner, he ought to denounce Lehman, too, and it noted that Morris and Lehman were conominees on the Liberal ticket and that fusion makes strange bedfellows.

That dinner, incidentally, resulted in the *Sun*'s getting the pictorial scoop of the campaign: *Sun* chief photographer Joe Lyons was on hand with his camera to get pictures showing Erickson, O'Dwyer, and Lehman in a group. The *New York Post* was for Morris and Lehman, and the verbal battle between O'Dwyer and *Post* publisher Dorothy Schiff will be referred to later. So much for the editorial positions for and against the candidates. How did the newspapers report the activities of those candidates in their news columns? We made a statistical survey during the week before election day—made a measurement of the amount of space given to reporting the speeches and activities of the major candidates.

We confined our measuring to stories in the late editions of the morning and afternoon papers; polls, editorials, and comments by columnists were not included. Here are the findings: In the *Times*, which was for Morris and Dulles, Morris got slightly more news space than O'Dwyer did, but Lehman did a little better than Dulles. Of all the city's newspapers, the *Times* gave the most news space in this period to the candidacy of Vito Marcantonio, with the exception of the *Compass*, which was supporting Marcantonio editorially. The *Herald Tribune* gave its favorite candidates, Morris and Dulles, a little more news room than it did their opponents, and Marcantonio didn't do nearly as well there as he did in the *Times*. The *Daily News* made its traditional battle page available to all candidates and printed generally well-rounded stories about them, although using very few individual reports. In the few special stories it did print, the *News* gave more space to O'Dwyer and Lehman than it did to Dulles, Morris, or Marcantonio, although it was editorially supporting Dulles and straddling the mayoralty issue. In the *Mirror*, O'Dwyer and Dulles dominated the headlines and the news space, and during the week of our measurement, Marcantonio was almost ignored. The *Compass*, on the other hand, was extremely generous with news space for Marcantonio and lumped the activities of most other candidates under a stock heading, "The Political Pot." The *World-Telegram* favored its selections, Morris and Dulles, in the news columns, and there was one interesting story which shows how you can use those news columns for editorials.

In the issue of November 2, a story was prominently displayed on the first page of the second section. It was headlined, "Vote campaign rich in double-talk and triple tripe," and it began as follows: "Silly statements are a dime a dozen in this year's New York state and city election campaigns, which have hit a new low in asininity." The story then went on to list some of the double-talk, triple tripe, and asininity, and curiously enough, all the samples quoted were from candidates which the *World-Telegram* was against or from their supporters. During the campaign, the *Telegram* got itself made the target of a million-dollar libel suit by Investigations Commissioner John J. Murtagh over a series of articles dealing with the sale of tax liens by the city. The first story said that although frauds were known to Murtagh thirteen months ago, no attempt has been made to recover any of the loss through civil action. The suit was filed after that first story appeared, but the paper continued to print the series, which was written by Murray Davis, one of the best-respected veteran reporters in the business. Commenting on the series, O'Dwyer said, "The story is not true, which is not unusual for the *World-Telegram*. When the *World-Telegram* hits below the belt, nobody is surprised. The reason is physical; it can't reach any higher."

That's pretty tough talk; it was NOT printed in the *World-Telegram*, which did, of course, report the law suit, and the rest of the papers reported the case in a variety of ways: Thorough reports in the *Herald Tribune*, which printed that quotation in full, and in the *Times*; adequate stories in the *Compass* and the *Sun*; nothing in the *Post*, *Mirror*, or *Journal-American*; and in the *News*, a mention that the suit had been brought against "an afternoon paper."

There were some other harsh words about and by the newspapers during the campaign, and a number of people got into the act. Concerning that story of the dinner attended by Erickson, O'Dwyer accused the *Sun* of trying to frame Governor Lehman, and he characterized the paper as a throwaway for the National Association of Manufacturers. The *Sun* replied in a dignified editorial that the mayor's anger was misplaced—that there were more important things for him to be indignant about.

There was another interesting pictorial incident during the campaign. Some weeks before the election, the Alfred E. Smith Memorial Foundation held a dinner at the Waldorf, and high dignitaries were on hand, all dressed up. Included among the dignitaries were candidates Lehman and Dulles, and as is usual at such functions, photographers were present to record the event. Now certainly the news feature of this was that the opposing candidates for the Senate were on hand to break bread amicably together on one occasion at least. So a photograph was made, showing, in the usual order, Governor Lehman (dinner jacket), Charles Silver (tails), Secretary of State Dean Acheson (tails), Governor Dewey (tails) shaking hands with Cardinal Spellman, and Senator Dulles (tails) looking on. That's the way the photograph appeared in the *New York Post*, but in the *Sun*, it had a different look. Governor Lehman had been eliminated from the picture, which simply showed Acheson, Dewey, Cardinal Spellman, and Dulles. Perhaps the *Sun* felt that Governor Lehman had been remiss in showing up in a mere dinner jacket with so many tails and white ties around.

But to return to more of those sharp words which featured the campaign. The high point of the vituperation was reached between Mayor O'Dwyer and Publisher Dorothy Schiff of the *Post.* The *Post* gave twice the news space to the candidacy of Morris than it did to O'Dwyer, and it used its news columns for a crusade against Dulles, too. Publisher Schiff accused Mayor O'Dwyer of threatening her through an intermediary and at an off-the-record news conference—a charge she did not elaborate. To this O'Dwyer retorted that the Schiff millions were trying to frame him and that he hoped the *Post* would never offend his nostrils by supporting him for anything. And Mrs. Schiff had an answer for that, printed in full in the *Post,* and any awards in a contest of billingsgate will have to go to her. She characterized the mayor as a "self-centered, self-indulgent, second-rate little politician" so frightened of losing his job that he has descended to the lowest possible level of political campaigning in order to retain it. Then Candidate Morris got into the act, as fully reported by the *Post*: Morris accused O'Dwyer of trying to gag the press and branded his attack on Mrs. Schiff as ungallant, untruthful, and despicable—a vicious attack on a woman whom Morris had known since she was a little girl. So far as we could find, the *Sun* was the only other newspaper to refer to this rhubarb between O'Dwyer and Mrs. Schiff, and of course, it, too, was having a set-to with His Honor. By contrast, the campaign story we liked best is one by Edward Zeltner, the *Mirror*'s Brooklyn columnist. The story is that weeks ago, before Morris uncorked his first salvo against O'Dwyer, he got a telephone call, and as reported by Zeltner, the conversation went like this:

> "Hello, Newbold, this is Bill O'Dwyer. Just learned your wife is ill. Anything I can do?"
>
> "Thanks, Bill. Mrs. Morris is coming along nicely. You've put me in a strange position; I'm going on the air in a few hours to rap the devil out of you."

> "That's all right, Newbold; we're in a campaign. Go ahead, and regardless of who wins, when it's over we'll have a drink together."

Now that's a heartwarming little story—makes you feel good all over that while men may go at each other hammer and tongs over public issues, they can yet keep their personal feelings out of it and have conversations like that one on a first-name basis. We liked the story so much that we tried to confirm it, on the theory that you see a lot of things in newspapers that you want to be sure about. Mayor O'Dwyer confirms the story, so does Morris, and we hope that the mayor and the losing candidate enjoy their drink very much whenever they get together. But what we'd really like to see would be Mayor O'Dwyer having a sociable drink with Dorothy Schiff of the *Post*, Keats Speed of the *Sun*, Lee Wood of the *World-Telegram*, Westbrook Pegler of the *Journal-American*, and perhaps one or two other newspaper people with whom the mayor traded compliments so vigorously during the campaign. That would make a picture worth space in anybody's newspaper, and you couldn't edit out a single character—it would be a unique gathering.

They've removed us from the lineup at this time next week. Instead of our play-by-play on the press, listeners will be treated to a broadcast of the California-Stanford football game—it's expected to decide one of the teams which will play in the Rose Bowl. But we'll be off the bench and back on the field week after next as usual, with some extra time to score the touchdowns and fumbles of the daily papers.

## February 4, 1950

Don Hollenbeck's last *CBS Views the Press,* like his first almost two and a half years earlier, focused on coverage by New York's newspapers of families on relief. In the process of evaluating news reports about the relief story, Hollenbeck asked—"in the name of public service"—when was something news and when wasn't it. He might have asked a similar question about the content of *CBS Views the Press.* When was it press criticism and when wasn't it? Hollenbeck's prize-winning *CBS Views the Press* served as the conscience of journalism in the world's most important media market. It critiqued the coverage by New York's major metropolitan dailies and other media of the most significant topics of the day. But Douglas Edwards's version of *CBS Views the Press,* which began on February 11, 1950, abandoned press criticism for a porridge of congratulatory notes, interviews with news correspondents, and such irrelevant puff pieces as a bow to the *Times* for helping fund Princeton's publication of Thomas Jefferson's papers. The *CBS Views the Press* written and narrated by Edwards, who commuted two and a half hours daily from New Canaan, Connecticut, lacked the firsthand feel for the city's newspapers so evident in the criticism by Hollenbeck, who lived in midtown Manhattan. It also lacked Hollenbeck's passion. For almost three months—from June 24 to September 16, 1950—Edwards's *CBS Views the Press* took a vacation. On June 23, 1951, Edwards broadcast for the last time, without indicating that *CBS Views the Press* would never be aired again. Appropriately, Edwards's lifeless version of the program died with neither a bang nor a whimper, only with silence.

ON OUR FIRST BROADCAST of this program, back in May 1947, one of the subjects we discussed was the current relief situation and the way it was handled by the metropolitan newspapers. We expressed an opinion that a section of the press had put on about as sorry an exhibition as it was capable of putting on and that its disclosures that a number of New York families on relief had been housed in hotels, in what was made to appear the lap of luxury, resembled a kind of newspaper lynching party. The immediate victims were almost 125 persons, housed in hotel rooms by the city's Department of Welfare on the grounds that they had not been able to provide adequate shelter for them elsewhere. That newspaper crusade was a success—if you can call a lynching a success. Almost every newspaper in town got into the act after the *World-Telegram* led the way, and the families were hustled from their rooms into condemned tenements and the city lodging house. A number of private welfare agencies came to the defense of the Welfare Department's position, but the fact was ignored by four of the nine papers reporting the story. And almost lost sight of in the fuss stirred up over the story was the fact that the great majority of the more than two hundred thousand persons on the city's relief rolls in 1947 got $1.31 a day for food, clothing, rent, and other needs. Shortly after this story, readers were introduced to the "Lady in Mink." New Yorkers must remember her as the woman with a young child and a shabby mink coat who was discovered on the relief rolls.

Last December we commented on the third appearance of the relief story. It all began on November 19, when the Department of Welfare announced that monthly payments would be reduced by two dollars a person, on the average. This affected nearly 320,000 persons who had been getting an average of $40.68 a month. The reason given for the reduction was a price decline in some basic foods and essential clothing. The *New York Times*, we said, seemed to be the only paper which gave the news story of the announcement adequate display. A few days later there was a new development—a release from a labor union which deals with the Department of Welfare on matters of its own personnel. Its survey, sent to all the newspapers, disputed the amounts of the reductions and said that they would be nearer three dollars a month and, in some cases, four. The newspapers ignored the analysis and, even if they suspected the source, made no attempt to check it—with one exception, the *New York Post.* About ten days after the analysis was made available to the newspapers, the *Post* printed a story by Joseph Kahn under the headline "$2 relief cuts more like $4 to most families." And Kahn kept turning up copy which verified the hardships most relief families faced. It was pretty much ignored by other papers, until the *Compass* took it up some days later. Our observation then was that perhaps it wasn't fun to play second fiddle—to follow along after the other fellow who had got on a story before you did. We were reminded that no newspapers in the days of the Lady in Mink minded playing second fiddle to the *World-Telegram*'s leading solo on the big luxury relief scandals of 1947.

But this latest chapter in the relief story did not end with our most recent discussion about the foibles of the papers' handling of it. The reductions were to become effective on January 16, at which time the Department of Welfare also was to change to a semimonthly payment of relief. The new payment system was ordered by the State Welfare Agency, which hoped to save three hundred thousand dollars a year in relief administration costs by the new system. Meanwhile, the *New York Post* continued its full-scale attack on the pending cuts, without much of an assist from the rest of the press. But on January 5, another voice was raised on the question. The *Daily Mirror,* which had had little to say about the matter in its news columns, took an editorial stand on the question. "Speaking of taxation," the *Mirror*'s editorial began, "we note that the entire phalanx of the left—from outright Communists to fuzzy-eyed 'liberals'—has lined up against Commissioner of Welfare Raymond Hilliard because he is trying to reduce the city's monstrous relief costs. In accordance with the requirements of the state, as well as the dictates of good administrative practice, Commissioner Hilliard will scale down relief allowances for food and clothing for the simple reason that prices in these fields have declined."

"Any cut in relief, however," the *Mirror* went on, "makes the commissioner fair game for the leftists, who delight in picturing him as a flint-hearted monster snatching food off the tables of little children and sick widows." "It is to every citizens' best interest," the *Mirror* concluded, "that he be firmly supported in his efforts."

Well, there are two extreme newspaper views on the matter—one fighting against what it considered the lowering of a substandard existence, the other approving the reductions and seeing political chicanery in objections to them. Whether you agree with either view or not, it was an indication to us that perhaps this relief story, as the deadline for the cuts drew near, was not going to continue to be a solo performance. We were wrong in our judgment by a few days, but on January 16, the day the reductions became effective, the story was back in the news. The publicity-wise Department of Welfare's press department released a story that morning which said that the city's relief rolls had shown a rise for the thirteenth month in a row and that Commissioner Hilliard had asked the state for help to set up a work relief project to allow "employables" on relief rolls to work for their relief checks. The *Times*, *News*, and *Mirror* ignored the fact that the new cuts were effective that day in their stories based on the release. The *Tribune*'s story put the fact right up in its lead. The *Compass* put a three-column, two-line head on its story which said, "Relief rolls up again: cuts in effect today." The *World-Telegram and Sun* noted the cuts in its story, and the *New York Post*, under a five-column headline on page 5, said, "Relief was cut today; meet some people who got hurt." Reporter Kahn's case histories in the story under that headline were given considerable space.

The next day the *Times* and the *World-Telegram and Sun* ran stories generalizing on what the reductions in assistance meant. They ran stories showing that 43 percent of all persons receiving relief were children and that those which would feel the cuts most were the group with jobs getting supplemental assistance and children in upper age brackets. The *Post* and the *Compass* continued to play the spotlight of publicity on the unfavorable results of the reduction. Then, a few days later, the federal, state, and city welfare representatives had a meeting. They agreed the 5 percent reductions were justifiable. All the papers reported their verdict in a more or less adequate display. The *Post,* however, dug a little deeper for its story and came up with quotes from a number of liberal leaders in civic affairs under a headline which said, "Civic leaders shocked at OK on relief cuts."

The next morning, January 20, the *New York Times* joined those voices—and the *Post*'s and the *Compass*'s—in a hard-hitting editorial which said in part, "We are not surprised by the unanimity with which the welfare conference of city, state, and federal officials found that the newly effective cuts in food and clothing grants were justified by price declines. State and city were long since known to have been in full agreement on them, and the federal government seems to have been present more as an observer than as a maker of policy."

"But, although we were not surprised by the conclusions," the *Times* went on, "we must say we are not happy over it. We are disappointed, for one thing, in the absence of any misgiving on the part of any conferee as to the adequacy of specific grants for nonfood, nonclothing items. . . . The conference relies on the generalization that, since food prices continue to fall, there is a margin for individual management." "This blandly assumes," the *Times* said, "that the food allowance is too large now, after the cuts, a conclusion we cannot bring ourselves to swallow. We are apparently making life pretty ghastly for some children and old people."

The editorial was apparently prompted by the findings of *Times* reporter Lucy Freeman, whose interviews with typical relief families appeared in the same issue of the *Times* under the head, "Relief cuts leave a wake of misery." That afternoon the *Post* found another bug in the new system of relief payments. Its three-column headline read, "Relief families hit hard by cuts face evictions under new payment plan." The story said that hundreds of relief families were threatened with eviction from their homes for nonpayment of rent since the department's semimonthly payment policy became effective. Previously, the story pointed out, relief checks were sent out on the first of the month, enabling families to pay their rent on time. Now, the story said, landlords were objecting to receiving the rent in two payments.

The *Mirror* continued to give the relief story attention in its editorial column. In an editorial on the twenty-first of January, it continued to take the opposite point of view from those expressed by the *Times* and the *Post.* The editorial said in part, "The big business of giving relief to New York's deserving needy cannot be run by picket lines, protests, or Communists and left-wing manifestore." The *Journal-American* paid little attention to the story one way or the other, then things generally quieted down in most of the papers—the exceptions being the *Post* and, to a lesser degree, the *Compass.* But last Monday the story was back in the news again in some sections of our press. The *Times, Tribune,* and the *Compass* ran another story based on a Department of Welfare release. The story said that Commissioner Hilliard had issued an announcement in defense of the 5 percent cut on the grounds that food prices were off 13.7 percent since June 1948. We didn't see the story anywhere else, but that afternoon the *World-Telegram and Sun* hit the newsstands with a three-column, two-line, front-page headline which said, "Relief thousands facing eviction." Its subsidiary headline said, "New payment plan raises rent crisis; city may advance $1,500,000 in aid." The next day the *Times* and the *Post* carried that story, too—the story the *Post* had had first crack at some ten days before the city decided to help. But the fact that the story found its way into the *Times* and the *World-Telegram* is to be praised, and the fact that both these papers joined with the *Post* and the *Compass* in giving their readers some chance to judge for themselves on the other side of the relief story is a step in the right direction in this ever-continuing story.

And now, as was announced last week, I'm turning over *CBS Views the Press* to new management—an increase of work makes it impossible to do full justice to a program which requires as much concentrated effort as this one does. Douglas Edwards and Jim Burke are taking over from me and Edmund Scott on the main part of the job, which is, of course, a cooperative venture by the CBS news room. Doug, with my congratulations, you are now the producer of *CBS Views the Press*, and I'd like to repeat what I said last week—that I think you'll find it just about the most stimulating and challenging assignment you've ever taken on.

EDWARDS: I'm sure of that, Don, but there's a piece of news tonight that you passed up and that I'm going to report now. *CBS Views the Press*, over a period of three years, has collected a lot of awards under your production of it—Peabody, Newspaper Guild, *Billboard, Variety*—and now there's another one. You've been awarded one of the George Polk memorial awards by Long Island University; they set up the award system in memory of our CBS colleague who was killed in Greece on his job as a correspondent. The awards are primarily in the field of journalism, and this year, for the first time, the university added a special category of press criticism because of this program's close relationship to journalism. My congratulations on another trophy, Don, and good luck.

HOLLENBECK: And good luck to you, Doug, and collect some for yourself.

The newspapers made much of her in great ink-letting headlines during the investigation, which resulted from the earlier newspaper crusade, and the press had a wonderful time with human misery during this period. However, their efforts forced a major shake-up in the department, where admittedly there was room for improvement in the job being done, even though the Lady in Mink was found to be eligible for the help she was receiving.

February 4, 1950

The relief story, like the conditions that make relief necessary, apparently will always be with us. Because just about a year ago this month, another relief scandal broke in the news—one more justifiable, we thought, than the previous one. This time the *New York Post* started the story. Its city desk had been receiving complaints from persons seeking relief that they were being made to wait, in some cases, more than a month before any help was given them by the Department of Welfare. Reporter Joseph Kahn was assigned to the story by editor Paul Sann. Kahn's story reported that the department was advising the destitute persons to borrow, stretch their food, and to go to their friends for immediate assistance. And finally, he wrote, the department was behind in its investigations by more than three thousand cases. But where two years before the papers hardly let an edition go by without howling in concert about the relief scandal, it was rather different this time. Not a single newspaper bothered to follow the lead of the *Post* and get to work on the story—a story which resulted in considerable commotion around town, with lots of prominent people and organizations voicing opinions. This made us wonder—in the name of public service—just what journalism was all about. When is something news and when isn't it?

# Index


Abbenante, John, 50
Abbott, Fred, 140
ABC, x
Acheson, Dean, 115, 125, 146
Adams, Phelps, 3
African Americans, 9–12, 65–69; Civil Rights Congress and, 126–32; Communism and, 126–32; *New York Age* and, 87–89; Ray Sprigle on, 78–85
Aidala, Arthur, 84–85
Andrews, Bert, 90, 92, 93, 109
Angell, Roger, 52
anthropology, 64–69
anti-Communism. *See* Communism
ape-man, 64–69
Arab-Jewish relations, 53–55
Argyris, Constantine, 60
Arm, Walter, 14
Arpad (cartoon character), 15
Associated Press, 6, 11–12, 29, 92, 100, 107, 123, 124, 138, 139, 140
athletes, 14
atomic energy, 17, 18–22, 121, 133–34

Bacall, Lauren, 25, 28
Baer, Betsy, 53
Baer, Stanley, 53
Baldwin, Hanson, 120
*Baltimore Sun*, 92
Barber, Mary, 60
Barber, Stephen, 60
Barrymore, Lionel, 99
Baruch, Bernard M., 40
*Bee-News*, ix
Belmont Stakes, 8
Benet, William Rose, 52
Bennett, Julie, 90
Benny, Jack, 2
Berger, Oscar, 101
Bigart, Homer, 57–60
*Billboard*, 155
Bird, Robert S., 7, 71
Black, Hugo, 81
Bogart, Humphrey, 25, 28
Bourke-White, Margaret, ix
Bourne-Vanneck, Richard, 87
Boyle, Vincent, 127
Brannan, Charles, 137
Brecht, Bertolt, 25
Brewster, Ralph Owen, 31
Bromfield, Louis, 99
*Bronx Home News*, 88
*Brooklyn Eagle*, 142
Broun, Heywood, 116
Brown, George Rothwell, 98
Brown, Harold, 111
Bullitt, William Marshall, 115
Burdett, Winston, 56
Burke, Jim, 155
Burley, Dan, 88–89
Bush, Godwin, 11–12
Bykov, Boris, 113
Byrnes, Gene, 53

California Committee on Un-American Activities, 127
*Carmen Jones*, 40
*CBS Views the Press*: awards won by, xi, 141, 155; coverage of motion-picture industry by, 25; criticisms of, 33–34; Douglas Edwards on, xi; Edward R. Murrow and, viii, x–xi; final broadcast of, 149–56; first broadcast of, 1–8; and hiring of Don Hollenbeck, viii, x–xi; revival of, xii–xiii; structure and purpose of, vii
Chambers, Whittaker, 109–17
Chandler, Douglas, 14
*Chicago Daily News*, 60
*Chicago Daily Tribune*, 102
*Christian Science Monitor*, 60, 93
Church, Francis P., 17
Churchill, Winston, 7–8
Civil Rights Congress, 126–32
*Clarion*, 70
Clark, Tom, 126, 127
Coates, Robert W., 52
Cold War, 118–26
Collingwood, Charles, xii, xiv
Colman, Ronald, 67
*Color Blind* (Halsey), 9
comic strips, 15, 23–24, 53
Communism, 3, 17–21, 76; freedom of expression and, 30–31, 92–93; in Greece, 56, 60–63; Hiss-Chambers trial and, 109–17; McCarthyism and, xiii–xiv, 70; motion-picture industry and, 25–30, 32; Paul Robeson and, 126–32; public fear of, 118–25; sabotage and, 31
*Compass*, vii, 119, 121, 131, 132, 144, 145, 146, 151–53, 154
Conklin, William R., 111
Conniff, Frank, 28
Cook, Fred, 15
Cooper, Kent, 92
Cronkite, Walter, xv
Crosby, John, xii, 1, 73
Crosley, George, 113
Curran, Joseph, 13

*Daily Worker*, vii, 93; on atomic energy, 20; on flying saucers, 23; letters to the editor and, 53; on public transportation, 6–7; on racial discrimination, 12
Daly, William Jerome, 6
Daniell, Ray, 60
Davidson, Carter, 54–55
Davis, Murray, 145
Dechene, J. M., 83
Desmond, James, 111
Deutsch, Albert, 4, 37
Dewey, Thomas E., 94–101, 102–3, 105, 146
Diamond Horseshoe, 40–41
*Dick Tracy*, 23–24
Dies, Martin, 116
discrimination. *See* racial discrimination

Donovan, Robert J., 12
*A Double Life*, 67
Dubinsky, David, 8
Dulles, John Foster, 115, 120, 143, 144, 146

Edel, Leon, 14
*Editor & Publisher*, 7, 33, 48–49, 94, 105–6
Edwards, Douglas, xi, 149, 155
Ehrenburg, Ilya, 58
Eisenhower, Dwight, xiii
Eliot Houses, 14
embedded journalists, 133–38
Endiner, Robert, 101
Erickson, Frank, 144, 146
Ernst, Morris, 52
espionage, 109–25
Euwer, Anthony, 77
Ewing, Oscar, 137

Fairfield, Cicily Isabel. *See* West, Rebecca
flying saucers, 22–23, 86
Fowle, Farnsworth, 54, 55
Fowler, Gene, 46
Fowler, H. W., 112
France, Shirley May, 138–40
Frankfurter, Felix, 115, 116
freedom of expression, 30–31
freedom of the press, 39, 69
Freeman, Lucy, 153
*Freewoman*, 70
Freidden, Seymour, 60
Friendly, Fred, viii, xi
Furman, Bess, 137

Gilmore, Dan, 140
Goldstein, Nathaniel, 128
Gould, Jack, 8
Grafton, Samuel, 49
Greece, 56–63
Greeley, Horace, vii
Griffin, William, 52
Griswold, Dwight, 57–58
Groves, Leslie R., 133
Gude, John, x

Haas, Victor, ix
Halsey, Margaret, 9, 76; *Color Blind*, 9
Hart, Lorenz, 40
Hayes, Arthur Garfield, 52
*Hear It Now*, xi
Hearst, William Randolph, viii, ix, xi, xiv, 48, 51–52
Hecht, Ben, 46
Hemingway, Ernest, 45
Hewitt, Don, xii
Hickenlooper, Bourke B., 18–21
Hilliard, Raymond, 151, 154
Hillman, Sidney, 8
Hiss, Alger, 109–17
Hiss, Pricilla, 112
Hodges, Gilbert T., 17
Hollenbeck, Anne, x
Hollenbeck, Don: on Alger Hiss, 109–17; awards won by, xi, 155; on Billy Rose, 40–47; Communism and, 17, 70, 118–25; criticisms by, 33–39; criticisms of, xiv, 1; death of, xiv–xv; departure of, from

Hollenbeck, Don (*cont.*)
*CBS Views the Press*, xi; on discriminatory coverage, 8; education and training of, viii–ix; firing of, from WJZ, x; hiring of, for *CBS Views the Press*, viii, x–xi; influence of, xii–xiv; last broadcast of, 149–56; *PM* and, ix; on Rebecca West, 70–77; on Westbrook Pegler, 86, 90–93; on William Laurence, 133–38; work of, in London, x
Hollenbeck, Zoë, xiv
"Hollywood Ten," 25
Holmes, Oliver Wendell, 30, 115
horse racing, 8
House Committee on Un-American Activities (HUAC), 20, 25, 26
housing, public, 1–3, 13–14, 16. *See also* welfare relief
Hutchins Committee, 39

Ikeler, Donald, 129, 132
*Il Progresso*, 142
Impelliterri, Vincent, 143
Ingersoll, Ralph, 43
International News Service, 140
Israel, 53–55

Jackson, Alan, xiii
Jacobs, Walter, 136
Jefferson, Thomas, 30–31
Jenkins, Burris, Jr., 21
*Jewish Day*, 142
Jim Crowism, 9–12, 66–69, 78–85
Jones, Lynn, 44
Jones, Vincent S., 45
*The Journalist and the Murderer* (Malcolm), 64
journalists: accuracy of, 8; African American press and, 87–89; anthropology and, 64–69; bias and politics of, 94–101, 141–48; Billy Rose and, 40–47; coverage of trials by, 109–17; embedded, 133–38; finance and, 7–8; freedom of the press and, 39, 69; kidnappings and murders of, 56–63; letters to the editor and, 48–53, 57–60, 76; manufactured news by, 25–32, 64–69; Pulitzer Prize and, 78, 79, 91–92; Ray Sprigle and, 78–85; and readers, 102–8; Rebecca West and, 70–77; and reliability of sources, 64; "scare-'em" reporting by, 118–25; and science, 133–38; technology used by, 83–85; word choices of, 33–39, 64–69
*Jumbo*, 40

Kahn, Joseph, 151–52, 156
*Kansas City Star*, 104
Kaufman, Samuel H., 109–10, 115–16

Kaye, Danny, 28
Kelleher, Walter, 131–32
Kendrick, Alexander, xi
Kenny, Nick, 51
Kent, Frank, 92
King, Carol, 114
Klies, Mrs. Len, 53
Knight, John S., 92
Krock, Arthur, 92, 135
Ku Klux Klan, 80–81, 127–28, 131

labor unions. *See* unions, labor
Laney, Al, 140
LaPolla, Ray, 130
Laurence, William, 133–38
Lehman, Herbert H., 143–44, 146
Lerner, Max, 98
letters to the editor, 48–53, 57–60, 76
Levin, Carl, 27
Lie, Trygve, 123–24
Liebling, A. J., 109
*Life*, 7
Lilienthal, David, 20
*London Evening Standard*, 82, 83
*London News Chronicle*, 60
*London Observer*, 60
*Long Island Star-Journal*, 142
*Los Angeles Examiner*, 22
Lough, Francis, 130
Louis, Joe, 100
Lucas, Jim G., 119–20, 125
Lyons, Joe, 144
MacArthur, Charles, 46
MacDonald, Walter, 4–5, 15, 16, 38
Mackey, Joseph, 14
Malcolm, Janet: *The Journalist and the Murderer*, 64
Manhattan Project, 133
Mann, Thomas, 98
Mannix, Joseph, 4
manufactured news, 25–32, 64–69
Marcantonio, Vito, 144–45
Marshall, George, 122
Maury, Reuben, 49–50
McCarren, Pat, 123, 124
McCarthy, Clem, 8
McCarthy, Joseph, xiii–xiv, 70
McKelway, Benjamin, 122
McLuhan, Marshall, 141
Meaney, Thomas F., 23
mechanization of society, 106–7
Miller, Joe, 100
Miller, Robert, 53, 54
Mockridge, Norton, 15
Moley, Raymond, 99
Moon, Henry Lee, 89–90
Morgan, Timothy, 46
Morris, Newbold, 143–44, 147–48
*Moscow Literary Gazette*, 46
Moses, Robert, 143
motion-picture industry, 25–30, 32
Mulholland, James V., 4–5
Murphy, Prosecutor, 115

Murrow, Edward R.: and *CBS Views the Press*, vii, 1; Don Hollenbeck and, vii, viii, x–xi, xii, xiv, xv–xvi; George Polk and, 56; on mechanization of society, 106; on Ray Sprigle, 79
Murtagh, John J., 145
Musel, Robert, 139–40

*Nation*, 101
National Association for the Advancement of Colored People (NAACP), 10, 11, 80
National Association of Manufacturers, 146
National Association of Radio and Television Broadcasters, xii
NBC, x
*The Nebbs*, 53
Nellor, Edward, 18, 19–20
newspapers. *See specific newspapers*
*Newsweek*, 93
*New York Age*, 66, 86, 87–89, 100
*New York Amsterdam News*, 66, 67, 68
*New York Daily News*, viii, 48, 71, 130–32, 143, 144–45; Billy Rose and, 43; on House Committee on Un-American Activities, 28; letters to the editor and, 48–51; on public transportation, 5–6; on racial discrimination, 10; "scare-'em" reporting by, 121
*New York Daily Mirror*, viii, 78, 131, 142; on Hiss-Chambers trial, 111, 114; on House Committee on Un-American Activities, 28, 29; letters to the editor and, 51; politics and, 97–98, 145, 147; on public transportation, 6; on racial discrimination, 10; relationship of, with readers, 48; "scare-'em" reporting by, 119, 121–25; technology used by, 83–85; on welfare, 4, 5, 37, 152
*New York Enquirer*, 52
*New Yorker*, 52, 67, 70–71, 109
*New York Herald Tribune*, vii–viii, 1, 14, 71; on atomic energy, 21–22; Billy Rose and, 41, 45; George Polk and, 57–60; Greek government and, 57–60; on Hiss-Chambers trial, 109, 111, 113–14, 116; on House Committee on Un-American Activities, 27, 29–30; letters to the editor and, 49, 52–53, 57–60; political coverage by, 96–97, 143, 144, 146; race and, 10–11, 12, 68, 81–82; Ray Sprigle and, 78, 81; Rebecca West and, 76; on rioting, 131; "scare-'em" reporting by, 119, 121, 122; on welfare, 5, 37
*New York Journal-American*, viii, xiv, 90; on flying saucers, 22; on Hiss-Chambers trial, 111, 114, 116; on House Commit-

tee on Un-American Activities, 28, 29; letters to the editor and, 51, 52; on organized labor, 8; political coverage by, 143; race and, 10, 13, 65, 68; relationship of, with readers, 48; "scare-'em" reporting by, 119, 121, 123–24; on welfare and housing, 2–3, 5, 14, 154; Westbrook Pegler and, 86

*New York Post*, vii, xv; on atomic energy, 20–21; on Hiss-Chambers trial, 116; on House Committee on Un-American Activities, 27–28; political coverage by, 95, 144, 146–48; race and, 10, 11, 12, 65, 68; on welfare, 5, 151–55, 156

*New York Star*, 95, 98, 141

*New York Sun*, vii, 1, 131; on atomic energy, 18–23, 24; on Communism, 17; on flying saucers, 22–23, 86; on Hiss-Chambers trial, 111; on House Committee on Un-American Activities, 28, 29; on Oak Ridge TN, 18–19; political coverage by, 141, 144, 146; race and, 10, 65, 68; on Santa Claus, 17–18; "scare-'em" reporting by, 119; on welfare and housing, 2–3, 5, 16, 154

*New York Times*, vii, viii, 92, 93; Arthur Krock and, 135; on atomic energy, 22; Greek government and, 60; on Hiss-Chambers trial, 110, 111, 112, 113; on House Committee on Un-American Activities, 27, 29–30; on Paul Robeson, 130–31; political coverage by, 96–97, 100–101, 103, 143; on public transportation, 6; race and, 10–11, 12, 68; "scare-'em" reporting by, 119, 120–21, 122–25; on welfare and housing, 4, 5, 150–55; William Laurence and, 133–38; Winston Churchill and, 7; word choices of, 35–36

*New York World-Telegram*, vii, 2, 33; on athletes, 14; on Hiss-Chambers trial, 115; on House Committee on Un-American Activities, 28, 29, 31; on organized labor, 12–13; political coverage by, 98, 143, 145–46; on public schools, 15–16; on racial discrimination, 11, 12–13, 65, 68; "scare-'em" reporting by, 119, 121, 124; on weather, 14–15; on welfare, 4–5, 16, 33–34, 38–39, 150

*Nieman Reports*, 50

Nimitz, Charles W., 51

Oak Ridge TN, 17, 18–22

O'Brian, Jack, xiv–xv

O'Donnell, John, 97

O'Donovan, John, 60
O'Dwyer, William, 4, 13, 37–38, 49, 141–48
*Omaha World-Herald*, ix
organized labor, 8, 12–13
Overseas News Agency, 60, 62

Palestine, 53–55
*Palestine Post*, 54, 55
Paley, William S., xii
*Paris Herald*, 140
Parsons, Geoffrey, 52
Pause, Bill, 15
*Peekskill Evening Star*, 127–29, 132
Pegler, Westbrook, 8, 86, 90–93, 98, 115–17, 148
*Pittsburgh Post-Gazette*, 78, 81
*PM*, vii, ix, 1, 14; on atomic energy, 20; Billy Rose and, 41, 43, 45; on Communism, 17; on House Committee on Un-American Activities, 27–28, 30; on public transportation, 6–7; race and, 11–12, 65, 68; on welfare, 4, 5, 37
political conventions, 70–77
politicians, 141–48
politics, 94–108, 141–48
Polk, George, 56–63, 155
*Post Home News*, 119, 131
Poston, Ted, 9
Poulos, Constantine, 60, 62–63
Price, Byron, 123, 125
Price, William, 6
public housing. *See* housing, public
public schools. *See* schools, public
public transportation. *See* transportation, public
Pulitzer, Joseph, 92
Pulitzer Prize, 78, 79, 91–92

racial discrimination, 9–12, 64–69. *See also* African Americans
Raleigh, Mildred, ix
Reagan, Ronald, 25
*Reg'lar Fellers*, 53
Reid, Ogden, vii
Reid, Whitelaw, viii
relief. *See* welfare relief
Reston, James B., 100, 103–5, 108
Reynolds, Quentin, 46
Rhatigan, Edward E., 3, 5
Richardson, Stanley, x
riots, 126–32
Roberts, Edward V., 118
Roberts, Roy, 104, 108
Robeson, Paul, 126–32
Robinson, Grace, 111
Robinson, Murray, 14, 15
Rodgers, Richard, 40
Roe, Billy, 100
Rogow, Lee, 44
Roosevelt, Eleanor, 115, 116
Roosevelt, Franklin D., 97, 143
Rose, Billy, 7, 40–47
Rosenberg, William Samuel. *See* Rose, Billy
Ross, Albion, 14
Runyon, Damon, 46

Sann, Paul, 156
Santa Claus, 17–18
*Saturday Review of Literature*, xiii
Scheele, Leonard, 137
Schiff, Dorothy, vii, 95, 98, 144, 147, 148
Schlacht, Harry, 51
Schmidt, Dana Adams, 60
Schoenbrun, David, 138
schools, public, 15–16
science journalism, 133–38
Scott, Edmund, viii, 155
Screen Actors Guild, 25
Scully, Frank, 26–27
Seacrest, Jessie, viii–ix
*See It Now*, xi, xiii, xv
Sentner, David, 28
Sharrow, Victor, 128–29
Shayon, Robert Lewis, xiii
Shrank, Helen, 44
Silver, Charles, 146
Simon, Eliav, 54
*60 Minutes*, xii
Smith, H. Allen, 15
Sokolsky, George, 98, 115
Sparks, Fred, 60
Speed, Keats, 1, 19, 21, 148
Spellman, Cardinal, 146
Sprigle, Ray, 9, 78–85
Staktopoulos, Gregory, 56
Stanton, Frank, xi
*Star*, vii
*Stars and Stripes*, x
Stevenson, Adlai, xiii
Stimson, Henry L., 115
Stix, Tom, x
*St. Louis Post-Dispatch*, 92
Stone, I. F., 20–21, 98
Stryker, Lloyd Paul, 115
Stuyvesant Town, 13, 14
Subotsky, Milton, 44
swimmers, 138–40
Swing, Raymond Gram, x

Taft-Hartley labor bill, 12–13
Thackrey, Dorothy. *See* Schiff, Dorothy
Thackrey, Ted, 95, 131
Thomas, J. Parnell, 29
Thomas, Norman, 98
Thomas, Victoria, 87
Thompson, Donald, 50
Thurber, James, 52, 67
Thurmond, J. Strom, 94, 104, 105
*Time*, 27, 44, 60, 102, 104, 109; Rebecca West and, 70, 71, 77; "scare-'em" reporting by, 121
Topping, Tom, 140
transportation, public, 5–6
Truman, Harry S., 19, 105; press coverage of, 94–101; "scare-'em" reporting and, 119; surprise victory of, 102; William Laurence and, 134, 137
Tuck, Jay Nelson, xv
Turcott, Jack, 6
Tynan, Kenneth, 70

UFOS. *See* flying saucers
unions, labor, 8, 12–13

United Press, 13, 60, 100, 119, 130, 139–40
*Utica Daily Press*, 45
*Utica Observer-Dispatch*, 45

Van Devander, Charles, 121
Van Paasen, Pierre, 98
*Variety*, 26, 155
Vermillion, Robert, 60
*Virgil*, 53

Walker, Danton, 2
Wallace, Henry, 76, 82, 94, 96, 97–99, 104
Wallace, Mike, xii
Walters, Jack, xi–xii
Washburn, Charles, 44
*Washington Star*, 122
*WCBS-TV Views the Press*, xii
weather reports, 14–15
Webster, Noah, 25–26
Wechsler, James A., 21, 116
*Weekly Block*, 86
Weiss, John, 37
welfare relief: average income from, 35, 37; housing and, 1–3, 13–14; press coverage of, 1–3, 149–56; and wealthy persons, 35–37
Werner, Ludlow, 66
Wershba, Joseph, viii, 109
West, Rebecca, 70–77, 78, 82–83
*We Take Your Word*, xi
Wheeler, John, 43–44, 53
White, E. B., 52, 53
White, Walter, 80
Williams, Gluyas, 53
Wilson, Woodrow, 77
Winchell, Walter, 4
Witt, Nathan, 114
women journalists, 70–77
Wood, Lee, 148
Wright, Frank Lloyd, 98
Wyer, Charles, 2
Wyer, William, 16

*You Are There*, xi
*Your Newspaper*, 142

Zeltner, Edward, 147
Ziegfeld, Florenz, 45
Ziegfeld Theater, 45
Zwicker, Ralph, xiii